Praise for *The Time*

"As an executive coach and entrepreneur, I am always seeking tools and investment opportunities to help increase my freedom and wealth. *The Time-Wealthy Investor* does just that, capturing the essence of real estate investing in a powerful and easy to understand way. It's not only a book about investing - it's a book about living life on your terms."

> - Lt Col (ret.) Waldo Waldman, *Peak Performance* speaker and author of the National Bestseller *Never Fly Solo*

"A great book for the buy-and-hold investor; manage without giving up all their free time. Being Time-Wealthy is something we should all strive for. Highly Recommended!"

> - Joe Fairless, Co-founder Ashcroft Capital, Best Selling Author, and Forbes Contributor

"A must-read for anyone looking to take their rental business to another level, and not spend all their time doing it. A great book to avoid creating a horrible job for yourself!"

> - Michael Blank, Author of Financial Freedom with Real Estate Investing, Apartment Builder, Investor, and Educator

"Whether you are a seasoned real estate investor, or just getting started, *The Time-Wealthy Investor* is a must-read! Mark Dolfini lays out a proven plan to leverage not just your money, but more importantly your time. Full of tips, strategies, helpful advice, and some crazy stories, this will become your real estate investing bible. I'm recommending it to all of my clients who own rental real estate."

> - Christine Luken, Financial Lifeguard, Speaker, and Author of *Manage Money Like a Boss: A Financial Guide for Creative Entrepreneurs*

Legal Disclaimer

This book is presented for educational and entertainment purposes. The author and publisher are not offering it as legal, accounting, or other professional services advice. While best efforts have been used in preparing this book, the author and publisher make no representations or warranties of any kind and assume no liabilities of any kind with respect to the accuracy or completeness of the contents and specifically disclaim any implied warranties of use for a particular purpose. Neither the author nor the publisher shall be held liable or responsible to any person or entity with respect to any loss or incidental or consequential damages caused, or alleged to have been caused, directly or indirectly, by the information or programs contained herein. Every business is different and the advice and strategies contained herein may not be suitable for your situation.

TWIPB2   TWVQ   TWBB   TWTTW

Landlord Coach Presents:

The Time-Wealthy Investor 2.0

Your Real Estate Roadmap to Owning More, Working Less, and Creating the Life You Want

By Mark Dolfini

About the Second Edition:

The honest and authentic feedback an author receives from their first book can be harsh. Words so hard to hear they could seemingly knock the bark off a tree. However, in order to make a good book among one of the greats, that sort of feedback is entirely necessary. Though largely positive, the feedback I received from the first edition of The Time-Wealthy Investor made me realize that the original needed some refining.

This second edition presents the elements in this book more congruently with the information in my full-day and weekend seminars. While the substance is largely the same, the presentation and format are a little different. Through multiple seminars, I adopted a more palatable approach that I refer to as the "VIP Paradigm" – Vision, Infrastructure, Process. The "Process Model" is still the same behavioral model as before, specifically Process-Expectation-Behavior, or PEB for short.

A few other elements of the book have changed, but beyond some simple editing mistakes that were missed – as annoying to a published author as a mosquito is to a tent camper – the only other alterations were updates to websites and vendors I have found to be helpful.

My goal is to make a much-improved roadmap for the reader. I hope I've delivered that for you.

Dedication

To all those who dared to try, and didn't confuse failure for defeat. To those who expected failure and embraced it. And to those who failed, and failed forward. You are my heroes.

Table of Contents

Introduction

Love, and do what you like.

– Saint Christopher

Financial wealth is attractive, no question about it. Unfortunately, it's often confused as the destination, rather than the vehicle – the means to an end – so to speak. If you consider what Time-Wealth means, that is, the ability to control one's calendar, then you might consider there being no greater wealth than Time-Wealth. You can borrow money and objects, but no one can borrow time. Time is universal – it is the great equalizer. Time applies to all of us without preference or reservation, even though it's so often wasted on dross and inactivity. I would argue Time-Wealth is the greatest, most fantastic wealth to be achieved.

To be among the Time-Wealthy is to have the freedom to do what you want rather than being a slave to how you produce income. Many people hope to get to this state of nirvana, this Promised Land, by achieving financial wealth. I will argue that this is the wrong target. Certainly, financial wealth is a great intermediate goal, and a necessary component to achieve Time-Wealth. But given our finite time on this spinning rock, shouldn't the ultimate goal be the ability to control your time so you're not spending every waking hour devoted to income generation? It should seem reasonable to say yes, but many people spend an awful lot of energy arguing otherwise.

The purpose of this book isn't to convince you of the importance of Time-Wealth; you will have to come to that conclusion on your own. No, the purpose of this book is to help you create capacity in your life - what you do with that excess capacity (read: time) is up to you. If you have chosen to invest in real estate as the vehicle to get you where you want to go, this book will help you operate your rental business without spending all your time doing it.

Investing in real estate is nothing at all like the promises made on late-night infomercials. Promises of financial-wealth are prolific, yet, they make little mention of Time-Wealth. Instead, we are shown flashes of beautiful people driving fast cars and living in homes so big they curve with the earth. Meanwhile, us "fools" toil in our daily lives. Many of us know the truth about these infomercials, but it's so hard to look away. The lure is simply too great. While financial security is certainly an ingredient of Time-Wealth, it's not the only part. Given our limited time on this planet, I find it sad that people collectively spend billions of dollars aiming at the wrong target.

Let's face it, your rental property, whether you have one or 40, is simply not an investment you can buy and never think about again. At least, not if you want to be successful. Certainly not if you want to be able to control your calendar. When you're buying a rental property, you're buying a business in the truest sense. You have a location, customers, vendors, revenues and expenses, and all the things resembling most other small businesses. So, let's just call it what it is, a business.

Once you shift your thinking to this paradigm you'll see the need to manage and operate your real estate business in a way that is consistent and scalable. Otherwise, all you've done is purchase a job for yourself; a miserable job that no one in their right mind would want. A job which allows you little to no time off, no ability to get sick or go on vacation, and causes nausea every time your cell phone rings. It may be exciting at first, but having your tenants call you whenever they feel like it gets old very quickly.

Being able to achieve time-wealth involves building a scalable and sustainable business that doesn't cost a fortune to operate. Such a framework must be intentional and does not involve things like downloading leases from places on the internet from a state whose laws you don't know. Nor would it include using tenant applications from somewhere else with no consideration to your existing infrastructure, risk tolerance, or fair housing laws.

Whether you own rental properties or not at this point, we're going to stay away from this sort of nonsensical thinking. Instead, we will create an intentional business framework that will prevent the frustrating conversations with residents which go nowhere and avoid activities that don't move you closer to where you want to be in life. The whole idea is to keep you from ever uttering the words: "Remind me again... why did I buy this (insert expletive) rental property?"

> **The desire for gold is not for gold. It is for the means of freedom and benefit.**
>
> **- Ralph Waldo Emerson**

In this book, you will learn how to set up a system that enables you to have a life. A good life – one that is better tomorrow than where you're at today. A life of purpose and intention. A life that excites you. That's the real reason, I suspect, you got into the rental real estate business in the first place – time freedom which enables the pursuit of other interests.

There is so much more to life than making money, namely having time to spend with your loved ones and doing that which excites you. This should be your number one priority, not spending countless hours being frustrated, or feeling as if you're being run by your real estate business.

What to Expect

This is not a book of the latest tips and tricks on being a landlord. On the contrary, this book will show you how to build a scalable real estate rental business that can operate without your constant oversight and input. To do that, you will learn, in depth, the Vision-Infrastructure-Process (VIP) Paradigm I've taught to many of my clients.

Starting with Vision, we uncover where you want to go. Specifically, if you thought of your business as a vessel, where would you want your real estate business to take you? Obviously you want a better life, we all do, but what does that mean for you? Having clarity in your Vision is critical before you can move on to the next piece; Infrastructure.

A sound infrastructure is something you'll need for a sustainable and scalable real estate business. From that base of infrastructure, you can craft procedures and policies for your business based on your personal skill set, financial situation, and desired level of involvement using the Process portion of the VIP model. The result is a real estate business which can be managed with limited involvement.

I'm not telling you it's going to be easy. I'm telling you it's going to be worth it. - Art Williams

Foreword

What then is freedom? The power to live as one wishes.

- Marcus Tullius Cicero

Roman Philosopher, Politician, Statesman

Some of us learn by doing, in spite of what we're told. I was the kid who touched the stove until I got burned, despite my mother's warning. Even as an adult, I often have to test the validity of a "Wet Paint" sign. As if somehow "the man" was trying to trick me and I have to prove him wrong.

I often think back to what got me into real estate in the first place. The lure of being my own boss and controlling my own destiny fascinated me. It often confused me as to why people saw a typical 8-to-5 job as less risky than owning and running their own business. The idea that your destiny is somehow safer in the hands of someone else – a boss, supervisor, or owner of a company – has always been foreign to me. I suspect if you're reading this book that to some degree you feel this way too.

This book is designed with a course mindset, and as such, much will be learned outside of the reading and from the process of the work itself. Yes, this will take effort beyond just reading the words. I will pass along concepts which have worked for me, but it will up to you to implement them in a way that will work best for you. In the end, having a business that provides you a steady stream of sustainable income that runs without your constant supervision will make it all worth it.

You may already own one or more rental homes.   If not, I congratulate you for being so proactive. Laying the groundwork for a business in advance makes much more sense than trying to backfill it as you go. I wish I did it that way, but being hard-headed, I chose the much more difficult and expensive route. Pretty much the way I learned as a kid. If you do own property, this book is going to help you identify the weakest areas of your business framework and enable you to get your weekends back.

What This Book is Not About

This is not a book about buying rental properties with no money down, or other such gimmicks. Nor is it about flipping properties, beating up the banks on the next foreclosure, analyzing your next deal, or determining ROI's, capitalization rates, and other financial measures.   This doesn't mean these subjects are unimportant, they're just not the purpose of this book. To you financial-metric nerds out there, put away the pitchforks and calculators. There are plenty of references to such things on this book's companion site www.LandlordCoach.com/twiBook.

A Small Business Analogy

Let's pretend you and I purchase a McDonald's restaurant, somewhere in America, but well outside the network of people in your hometown. We get a great deal on the building, and even with the worst-case cash flow projections, we're sure to make a decent return on our money. The only issue is we're buying the McDonald's with no Point of Sale system, training manuals, procedural manuals, checklists, mops or buckets. Additionally, once the business is sold, all of the employees leave to work somewhere else. Basically, we have bought a building with no clear way in which to operate it as a business.

Given this scenario, what do you think our first day of operations is going to be like? Trying to run this business without the proper infrastructure conjures up visions resembling the final moments of The Hindenburg.

Obviously for a busy McDonald's, running an operation this way would be impossible. Without some sort of business framework in place, all we've done is create a horrible job for ourselves – taking all the orders, making the burgers, placing all the pickles and onions, running the registers, and cleaning the bathrooms. As real estate investors, this analogy is one we want to avoid, buying properties with no systematic way to run them. This book will help you with the framework you need for your real estate business.

Chapter One

The Time-Weary Landlord

Beware the barrenness of a busy life.

- Socrates

Overworked, stressed out, and broke, Jack is a Time-Weary Landlord. He starts his weekend sitting in his home office staring at the stack of papers and unopened mail that has amassed on his desk, unsure of even where to start. He used to consider himself good at paperwork until the sheer volume of it made this piece of life his own little nightmare. It's 7 o'clock on Saturday morning, and while his friends warm up for a round of golf, Jack stews about all the things he's got to accomplish for his rental business today. After many weeks of declined invitations, his friends don't even bother to ask him anymore. Jack can hear them from his window across the street, conversing and laughing, he stands to watch the car doors close one at a time, and off they go.

Jack plops down in his chair and starts going through the mail and the stack of paperwork. He opens a utility bill the tenant was supposed to put in their name more than two months ago. Next, a property tax bill. After that, a post-dated rent check from the one tenant who sends her rent in advance. A few minutes after eight, his cell phone rings and Jack's stomach sinks. He's grown to hate the sound of his cellphone, mostly because nearly every time it rings it's more bad news about one of his rentals or drama from one of his tenants. At work, his ringing cell phone has become such an issue it's become a topic of frequent conversation among his coworkers. In fact, just this past week, Jack's boss pulled him aside to discuss the excessive amount of time spent on non-work activities and distractions. Jack's rental business is running his life.

Taking a breath and answering his phone, Jack promptly goes on the defensive as the tenant on the other end launches into a tirade about her broken refrigerator. Thirty minutes, four apologies, and one promise to make things right, Jack hangs up the phone frustrated and defeated. "It's not even 9 o'clock yet!" He stews out loud. He'd already contacted the appliance repairman and thought this had been handled. Or, had he forgotten? Being so distracted by things between the rental business, his day job, and his home life he can't remember if he's made the call or not.

Either way, considering it's Saturday and the possibility of getting a repairman to fix the problem is pretty slim, he's now faced with the reality of his tenant going the rest of the weekend without a refrigerator. "She has two small children," he reflects; the thought makes him uneasy. He had been called a "slumlord" before, among other things that polite people don't repeat. While he felt it was unjustified at the time, the truth was obvious. Going from one crisis to the next, Jack was constantly in reaction-mode. He knew deep down he deserved the criticism for being slow to respond to the needs of his tenants.

He really wanted to do the right thing even though he had no idea how he was going to afford it. He had some credit left on his Lowes account, so he could buy a new one and have it delivered. All the while, Jack contemplated how he was going to even begin to pay for all these expenses which were now completely out of hand. The repair of a refrigerator would likely have only cost $200 or so, now he was looking at over $500 to purchase a new one.

"If you don't put a value on your free time, someone else will"

Jack spent the rest of the morning and most of his afternoon going through paperwork, calling on tenants that owed money, running a few errands, stopping by a few of his properties, and addressing more maintenance requests before making it back to his office again. Before he knew it, the sun began casting shadows in his office as dusk approached. "How in the world is it 6 PM already?" Frustrated, aggravated, and feeling completely overwhelmed, Jack decided to call it a day. He was supposed to go on a dinner date with his wife. With so much on his mind, maybe they could just stay in, order a pizza, and watch a movie. She always seemed to be understanding when it came all the responsibilities of his rental business, but he also knew that everyone had their limit.

Jack was excited when he first got into this business. His 14 rental units were supposed to give him a measure of financial independence and control over his life, but the reality has been the exact opposite. The sad part of this story is that much of this could have been avoided.

Early on, Jack failed to identify the need to set up a basic business architecture that didn't require his constant attention. He wanted to self-manage his properties to save money, but in doing so he also failed to recognize himself as the bottleneck for all decisions to flow through. Causing a lack of scalability that stymied further growth and sucked up all his free time as he expanded his operation from one, to three, and then eventually to the 14 properties he now owns.

The key to avoiding problems like Jack's is to have a business framework that allows you to operate efficiently, effectively, and is scalable yet won't cost a fortune to operate. Scalability is crucial in an expanding operation because you need to be able to handle 20 rental units about as easily as you can handle two. Jack failed to recognize this which he now pays for in lost rents, unhappy customers, and lost leisure time. He also made the critical mistake of not placing enough value on his free time. As a result, his tenants did that for him. The trouble is, the value they put on his free time has become far below what Jack is worth, and he knows it. Remember, if you don't put a value on your free time, someone else will.

The Secret Freedom of Scalable Infrastructure

Jack learned things the hard way by not having his business in order. Not only by giving up his weekends, but also by becoming the point of congestion that prevents the efficient operation and expansion of his business. He's figured out that he needs a process that can grow and expand with his operation. Having a successful real estate business isn't as simple as buying a rental property, sticking an ad on Craigslist, and watching the money roll in. If you don't own rental property yet, I'm glad I could save you both money and headache from that misconception.

While there is much more than that to having a successful real estate operation which doesn't chew up all your free time, the secret really isn't that profound either. In fact, there really is no secret. At the core, it's simply developing an infrastructure and creating a business process in alignment with your vision for the future. It's the framework that will allow you to run your business and work so you can live, not the other way around. Read that last sentence again, it's important. If it's your vision to become the next Howard Hughes, or to have more free time to chase butterflies with your cocker spaniel, it's necessary to have a framework and system in place that is in complete alignment with your vision for the future and your tolerance for risk.

Consider this example: Say your vision is to travel with your family, where you spend an entire month sitting on the beach all day. An infrastructure that requires you to return emails and phone calls in a timely manner is not going to work well for you if you're sitting on the beach sipping fruity drinks with little umbrellas. In this context, make sure your vision is clear, and build an infrastructure in alignment with that vision.

"Work so you can live, not the other way around"

A Roadmap, not a Recipe, for Success

Before we dive in, I want you to consider this book as more of a roadmap than an exact recipe or do-this-then-do-that type of manual. It is meant as a guide from someone who has been down this road before you, but it will be up to you to fill in the fine details. Every situation is different, so trying to come up with every possibility you might face would not only be a waste of trees, it would stifle the creative juices within you, the entrepreneur. Besides, it's your business; make it your own!

Keep in mind, even the best roadmap isn't going to show every little pothole, road construction, detour, or roadblock along the way. As in life, all those things are temporary. Those little bumps and obstacles in our way need to be addressed in some way by going around them, over them, or in some cases, through them. This book is not just about being a better, more effective property investor; this book is your roadmap to a better life. Everyone's route is going to be a little bit different. It's up to you to decide exactly which route you take to get there.

Chapter Two

The Folly of the Entrepreneur

He who knows, and knows he knows, he is wise,
> follow him.

He who knows, and knows not he knows, he is asleep,
> awaken him.

He who knows not, and knows he knows not, he is a child,
> teach him.

He who knows not, and knows not he knows not, he is a fool,
> avoid him.
> - Ancient Proverb

I am not ashamed to confess that I am ignorant of what I do not know.
- Marcus Tullius Cicero

For those of you who have read Michael Gerber's book *The E-Myth Revisited*, this opening chapter may resonate with you. A good friend of mine observed my business struggles and suggested it to me. After reading it, I had to come to terms with what I considered to be the typical folly of the entrepreneur. Most entrepreneurs I know are very intelligent people. They have the ability to learn and figure out how to do most things. ***Need to update your website?*** A quick two-hour tutorial with your website designer and you're good to go. ***Need to learn to fix a dishwasher?*** A simple scroll through YouTube and you're an instant expert. Short of teaching your short-haired calico to load the dishwasher, there's not much the entrepreneur won't do, or at least try. I had to learn to be okay with the concept that just because I **can** do something, does not mean it's the highest and best use of my time.

In 2007, I decided to apply for membership in a BNI chapter, a weekly business networking group. For those of you not familiar with BNI, it's a networking organization with chapters all over the world. It helps people grow their businesses by asking for referrals to ideal customers. In addition, it helps develop you professionally. Not realizing it at the time, the latter of the two was much more valuable to me. I didn't know what I didn't know. Simply put, as in the Ancient Proverb, I was the Fool.

I felt as if I had much to gain and little to lose. Armed with a B.S. in Accounting from Purdue University, I had been in the working world for a few years and was just starting to develop myself professionally. I'd been involved with another business group previously where we discussed sales techniques and other business subjects, and, although helpful, it was small and loosely organized. BNI was much more intentional and structured, which, since becoming self-employed, were things my business was sorely lacking.

> *"Just because you can do something, does not mean it's the highest and best use of your time."*

Self-Employed vs. Business Owner

Not long after joining BNI, and in absorbing the teachings of *The E-Myth Revisited*, I understood the difference between being self-employed and being a business owner. Making the transition from the former to the latter required a complete paradigm shift and rewiring of my brain from the way I was doing things. My default mode was being action-oriented; this was not an easy period for me.

At the point of my awkward transition, I had amassed 92 rental units which equated to roughly $60,000 per month in rental revenues. This amounted to about $6 million worth of real estate, which I acquired through a hodgepodge of creative financing, wheeling, and dealing. I operated this without an office, just a truck with a power invertor and an adjustable stand for my laptop bought from a police supply catalog. I purchased an internet air-card so I could check emails, update my website, or review my bank account. With a printer in the back seat, I could print leases and other necessary paperwork. It was a mobile office that was efficient in some perverse way I suppose, but far from effective, and certainly not scalable.

In addition to this limited infrastructure, the only "process" I had in place was to put out fires. I was in constant reaction-mode and everything was done on the fly. I handled everything from the painting, cleaning, and advertising of my vacant units, to doing the showings for prospects. In addition, I somehow found time to do collections, file eviction notices, and show up in court. I took deposits to the bank, got the mail, paid all the bills, and reconciled the bank accounts. Somehow, I attempted to perform the maintenance on an ever-growing list of requests which once started as a gentle snowfall, had become a crushing avalanche. And my cell phone never stopped ringing. Ever.

I did it all, and it was pure chaos. I was being pulled in so many different directions I could do none of it well. The way I was managing my business was not only crippling financially, but I understood what it meant to be Time-Weary. It wasn't long after I learned how bad it could really get; being "Time-Bankrupt". I was being crushed by the weight of all the work, and it was only a matter of time before the house of cards fell. I had no endgame except to slog along for another 25 years when the mortgages would pay off and I could hire some help. If I didn't have a stroke first, of course.

My life was completely consumed by my business. I considered what I would do if, God forbid, something happened to one of my parents and I needed to take care of them. They both lived out of state and surely weren't getting any younger. Forget anyone else for a second, heck, what would happen if something happened to me? I mean, dozing off on a ladder after three hours of sleep the night before was not that far-fetched. Scary thoughts like these were as pervasive as they were dangerous. I didn't know the answer, but I knew something had to change. At least now I knew there was something I didn't know. Referencing the Proverb, no longer the fool, I was a child.

The only true wisdom is in knowing you know nothing.

- Socrates

A Brief Moment of Clarity

One morning, after a particularly punishing series of days, I arrived at my BNI meeting a few minutes late. The networking portion of the meeting started promptly at 7AM, and my late arrival had become part of my routine. One of the members of the chapter owned a restoration business where the meeting was held. Whether Jeff knew it or not, I had adopted him as my mentor. Since I'd met him, I was impressed by how he and his wife ran their operation of more than 40 employees and multiple locations. I was coming in the door and Jeff stood, coffee in hand, ready to start the day. I must have looked more haggard than usual. He stood, smirking, not saying anything.

Breaking the silence, Jeff greeted me,

"Good morning! How's it going?"

"Oh, not bad; really busy!" I fired back eagerly, as if "busy" was a badge of honor to be worn proudly.

"You look a bit ragged this morning." Jeff noted, "What's got you so busy?"

"Well, just a little bit of everything I guess," I answered. "I'm doing all the maintenance on my units, plus all the leasing, all the showings, all the paperwork, and the rent collection. I guess I'm just running a bit too hard right now. It will slow down… someday." I smiled, seeking some approval from my self-assigned mentor.

Jeff smirked, I suspect knowing that I wanted him to be impressed. He thought for a second, took a deep breath and continued the conversation.

Nodding, he started slowly, "You do maintenance work for people, right?"

This was true. I started doing appliance repair, maintenance work, and other general handyman-type repairs as a side hustle for some of the people in my BNI chapter. I was very fortunate to be handy when it came to fixing most things.

"Yes, I do some appliance repair and other handyman-type work. Why?" I asked.

"And you charge what, $30 an hour for that service?" Jeff inquired.

I nodded in reply; at the time that was accurate.

Jeff, nodding back in response, continued, "So how much would you have to pay for a maintenance guy to do what you do?"

I paused for a second, because that thought had never crossed my mind. After a moment I answered, "I don't know, for the low-end stuff, painting and trash-outs, maybe $10 or $12 an hour".

"Well," he paused, "You realize that's exactly what you're paying yourself, right?"

That single statement sent me down a path that forever changed the way I looked at my business. For a moment, I didn't quite comprehend what that meant, but Jeff knew enough to stay silent and let that soak in. I could tell he truly wanted to help me. As this was marinating inside my head, I suspect my body language resembled something like the Hulk turning back into David Banner, the neurons in my brain rewiring themselves to this new paradigm.

Suddenly, the epiphany came, a moment of clarity.

"Holy (bleep)!" I said out loud, "No wonder I'm broke!" I laughed, but it really wasn't funny.

From a very basic math perspective, *I was costing my business money every time I did work that I could pay someone else to do cheaper.* This was especially true of the low-end type work such as painting, cleaning and general labor. I was costing myself $18 an hour by doing it myself ($30 minus the $12 I would have paid someone else to do it).

This is what is known as Opportunity Cost and it works like this: Opportunity cost is the event you have foregone to pursue an alternate activity. By doing the lower-end work myself, I was forgoing the opportunity to pursue higher-end work.

Here's an example if I did the handyman work myself:

$30 per hour times 10 hours equals $300 (money coming in)

I would make $300 in a day if I did all the work myself.

If I hired someone to help do the handyman work:

$30 per hour times 10 hours equals $300 (money coming in from an employee)

PLUS

$30 per hour times 10 hours equals $300 (money coming in from my work)

LESS

$12 per hour times 10 hours: -$120 (money paid out for labor)

EQUALS

$480 (I make from having someone else do the work)

In considering what happens when I do all the work myself, the Opportunity Cost:

Doing all the work myself $300

Less the money I could make with help ($480)

Loss per day Equals: ($180)

I was costing my business $180 per day per 10-hour period by doing all the work myself, a whole $900 every Monday through Friday. I still had to take care of all of the paperwork, collections, lease showings and other administrative duties, but at least this would provide me some much-needed breathing room and establish a point I could build from. Not only was I broke financially, but I was also suffering among the Time-Weary.

How was it that I had never figured this out? Well, given the role I had placed myself in as a constant fire-fighter, there was no way I was ever going to see it on my own. The problem was, I had not come to realize that even though I *could* do most things, not all activities were the highest and best use of my time. Thus, the folly of the entrepreneur, and in my case, being a Time-Weary Landlord.

Chapter Three

Rental Hell

To be tested is good. The challenged life may be the best therapist.
- Gail Sheehy, Author

Life's tough, but it's tougher if you're stupid.
- John Wayne

Fast forward a few years, and my business had evolved into not only managing my own rental units, but I was also operating as a property manager for other real estate investors. Like I had been, they were looking for relief from the landlording rat race they found themselves in. One day I got a call from an older couple that owned 25 units who were considering hiring a property manager. Nearly all of their properties were single family homes. The couple invited me to their office to tell them about our property management service and how we might be able to help them.

Their office, as it turned out, also doubled as their home. Nice but modest, I was welcomed warmly and offered a chair at the kitchen table. Taking a seat, I looked around to see family photos, pictures of grandchildren, fake flowers in vases, doilies, and uncomfortable-looking furniture you would expect to see in someone's grandparent's house. I offered a warm smile to the couple, "How are you today Mr. and Mrs. Jackson?"

The woman huffed in what seemed to be a well-rehearsed response, "Just another day in the rental business..." forcing a smile in return. I smiled, letting her know that I understood what she meant. "How long have you guys been doing this?" I asked. "Twenty-eight years," she said softly, "but we've only owned some of them for about fifteen or so." Raising my eyebrows, I was shocked by their level of experience, "I bet you've about seen it all then, huh?" I asked. Mrs. Jackson smiled politely, but she was in no mood to trade war stories.

Judging by the look on their faces, I could tell they were mentally beaten down. They were good people, that was evident. Unfortunately, being a good person does not excuse doing bad business. In fact, it's often worse because of the mental disconnect your customers have with their expectations of your behavior **because** you're a decent person. They see you and your business as one in the same. To that point, good people shouldn't do bad business. If someone feels as if they are being treated poorly, or even inconsistently, they are that much more negative when it comes to your business and the unpredictability they experience.

As we continued our conversation, I couldn't help but feel sad for the Jacksons. They felt helpless in their current situation. At one point I asked, "When was the last time you went out to dinner and didn't have to bring that?" pointing to the cell phone conspicuously placed on the table. Mrs. Jackson's eyes welled up, she knew that I understood their struggle. Almost to the point of tears, we talked about the last time they had a vacation, or even when they were able to see their grandchildren for a long weekend.

Mr. Jackson, who seldom spoke during our meeting, chimed in, "That's why we're just thinking of selling the units and be done with it."

"Interesting," I thought out loud, nodding as I considered what he'd said. I let a few moments go by before saying anything. Then I asked, "Do you have anything in particular you're planning on doing with the money?"

I felt it was a fair question, and it was clear that Mr. Jackson hadn't really given it any thought. "No, but I just want to be done with them." He barked back, pausing for a moment. "I want our life back." His wife was looking down at the table as he spoke. I found all this incredibly ironic because I didn't get much sense that the husband really had much to do with the rental properties. All the work was being done by his wife, and from what I could tell, she had been doing it all along.

Adding to much of the drama was that the Jacksons lived very close to all the rental units they owned. This gave their tenants near-immediate access to the Jackson's due to their rental office being about ten feet from their living room. Residents showed up at all hours of the day and night, dropping off rent, submitting work order requests, or to come by and complain about this or that. Of course, this also included people who were upset or angry about being evicted. Their process was a complete mess and they paid for it in comfort, leisure time, and privacy.

The really sad thing about this story is that the Jacksons were literally on the doorstep of the "Promised Land" that every landlord strives for. Nearly all of their 25 units were owned free and clear. They had enough in savings to pay off their mortgages and own all their properties outright. The units generated over $18,000 per month in revenues, well in excess of what they needed to cover their expenses, and could offer them a very cozy lifestyle when they figured in their Social Security and pension income.

Running their business with such a lack of vision and dearth of infrastructure had left them so emotionally compromised that they were willing to walk away from all they'd built over the previous two decades. Consider too the good chunk of tax money they'd owe to Uncle Sam when the properties were sold. The real tragedy however, was that they had no plan to replace the income stream once they got their lump sum of money from the sale of all their real estate. I felt as if I was watching someone get into a leaky lifeboat in shark-infested waters when there was no compelling reason to leave the ship.

The fact is that all of this indigestion could have been avoided. Whether they realized it or not, these problems were entirely their fault. The Jacksons failed to ever develop any sort of infrastructure that did not include them or their labor as they scaled up their rental operation. All they did was create a job for themselves, a job that no person in their right mind would have wanted. Needless to say, this is exactly where you don't want to end up.

Knowledge has to be improved, challenged, and increased constantly, or it vanishes.

- Peter Drucker

What You Need to Bring

Over the years, I've heard many investors talk about how difficult it is to be in the rental business. Life can be incredibly rough when you climb into any business without proper planning, so let's discuss how to get the most out of this book. There will be concepts introduced to you that you might already be doing and some that might be counter to what you're doing. My basic premise is if you have a policy in place that is effective I'm not about to tell you to stop. However, there will likely be other ideas you feel don't apply to you, or are just not relevant to your situation. Whatever the case, I want you to come to the table with a mindset that prepares you for success.

Instead of thinking, "This concept won't work," I'm going to ask that you approach each new idea with a paradigm of "How could I *make* this work?" If your approach to life is being skeptical of everything new until you have concrete evidence, this is going to be a very slow process. I know this to be true because I was "That Guy". Set aside your need to be "right". Keep an open mind and I promise you, not only will a whole other side of this business emerge, but a whole new life.

Most of the changes you will make to your business are not giant and sweeping but rather small and seemingly innocuous. However, like putting pennies in a jar, it will all start to add up. I ask that you put aside your preconceived notions of success or failure of a given concept before even giving it a chance to work. In writing this book, I had to do the same thing. We all need to keep learning, keep implementing, keep working and reworking, and keep doing. Don't let your current line of thinking hold you back. Constant learning prevents mental stagnation and continually moves us forward.

You are one decision away from a totally different life.

- Mark Batterson

The View of Life from a Hospital Bed

It was only a matter of time before my own particular house of cards fell. Like most dramatic stories, mine has the same "Jerry Maguire" moment as all the rest. It was during a particularly bad period in 2009 when everything around me was going to crap.

The economy had tanked, the labor market was in turmoil, and my personal life had been circling the bowl for a while too. Most of my renters at the time were the "buy-here, pay-here" type of individuals. About a third of them were out of work, and it wasn't long before I joined them in financial trouble. My monthly rent revenues went from over $60,000 to $30,000 simply because of employment problems experienced by my tenants. The same for the next month, and the month after that, and the month after that. My savings of $65,000 in cash had vaporized nearly overnight and I was a financial dumpster-fire.

I had no money for anything. Not only was every single one of my mortgages delinquent by 30 days or more, I barely had enough cash to buy paint and clean the units. I was, in one stage or another, at risk of losing every rental property I owned, along with my house, my car, and everything I had worked so hard for up to that point. Not surprisingly, all the back-to-back 22-hour days finally took their toll on me. My health suddenly became an issue when, what started out as a simple cold, developed into double-pneumonia.

Figuring I'd "tough it out," I only dragged myself to the hospital when I reached the point where slumping over the back of a chair was the only way I could breathe. At the ER, I was placed on a gurney in a triage room, gulping for air like a fish out of water. The nurse said she'd ordered a breathing treatment for me, and a respiratory therapist would be by to see me soon. At that point, she left the room.

I laid there alone. Panting, wondering, waiting; my breaths became more and more shallow. My situation was becoming desperate. I'd grown up with asthma, so I knew what it felt like to live breathing through a cocktail straw, but this was very different. Something was very, very wrong.

This hospital was newly constructed, and I later found out that the respiratory therapist who was supposed to bring me a breathing treatment didn't know where to find me. My flight crew training in the Marines taught me about the effects of hypoxic hypoxia, which is what happens when the body is being starved of oxygen. Most notably, the edges of my vision were becoming blurry, my hands and feet were tingling, and I was extremely drowsy. An odd, almost euphoric calm came over me. I remember thinking that this was how my life was going to end. I'd resigned myself to the fact that I could quite likely die right here on this bed, completely alone.

Lying on my side, the drowsiness overtaking me, I closed my eyes and felt myself drifting off. The sound of the door brought me back to awareness. Footsteps. Voices. More footsteps. The door again.

What I could piece together afterwards is that someone came into the room, noticed I was in a desperate state, and got the breathing treatment expedited. When the respiratory therapist arrived, if I could have mustered the energy, I would have unleashed some fury in her direction. I set that aside though; I was just happy to be getting oxygen again.

I spent the next three days in the hospital trying to clear my lungs of the fluid that invaded them. I wondered about all the things that were not getting done at work and felt guilty about all the things I could have been doing. I kept coming back to the conversation that my mentor and I had. I didn't know what I needed to do exactly or how to set it up, but I couldn't continue this madness.

My business desperately lacked infrastructure. It lacked systems and processes. At the very least, it lacked focus and intention. It lacked vision. From that moment in the hospital, I resolved to do one thing: I was going to make the transformation from self-employed individual to business owner. At least now I had a vision as to what that looked like. I finally had a direction to head in. It was time for me to wake up.

He who knows, and knows not he knows,

he is asleep, awaken him.

Chapter Four

Vision – Getting Clarity

Awakening is not a thing. It is not a goal, not a concept. It is not something to be attained. It is a metamorphosis. If the caterpillar thinks about the butterfly it is to become, saying 'And then I shall have wings and antennae,' there will never be a butterfly. The caterpillar must accept its own disappearance in its transformation. When the marvelous butterfly takes wing, nothing of the caterpillar remains.

- Alejandro Jodorowsky,

Director, Screenwriter, and Author

As I sat in my hospital bed with nothing but time and my thoughts, realizing that my problems of infrastructure and Time-Weariness were larger than me, I stared out the window considering what I needed to do. I decided to turn to two of the smartest and most resilient people I knew, my mother and my father.

My mother grew up in Scotland during The Blitz, and although she was too young to recall it, she remembered the stories my grandmother told her about how tough things really were. My mom didn't know any different, that's just how things were after the war. Food rationing and other resource shortages, it was all normal to her growing up.

My mom, smart and possessing a keen ability to get things organized, spent her professional career as a full-charge bookkeeper. I flew her in from New York to help me get things in order and offer an outside perspective. She spent a few days at my home office establishing for me a basic level of organization and a solid starting point from which I could build.

My dad on the other hand, armed with different tools and experiences, offered another perspective. A self-made man with just an eighth-grade education, he got to where he was with sheer grit. While not particularly well-educated, he's one of the smartest people I know. During the days of the Interstate Commerce Commission, he built a multi-million dollar trucking operation while Jimmy Hoffa and the Teamsters did all they could to strong-arm my father into unionizing. The stories my father told me about those times both fascinated and terrified me. He told me of the skirmishes they'd have with the union guys who frequently shot bullet holes into the trucks and trailers and slashed the tires of parked vehicles in their lots. In those days, that's how it was.

> "It was a different time then," he laughed, "you could never get away with the sort of stuff now that we did to those [expletive] Union guys." The smile drifted from his face, "But they were bullies, they had it coming to them."

> "They even had you kids followed home from school a few times. There was no place for that," he continued, "Plus if I'd have given in to them, they would have driven me out of business and left us and my employees much worse off."

My dad and I talked at length. Bits of knowledge and wisdom flowed from one story to the next. One of the less felonious and more relevant things I learned during those conversations was the key that allowed him to expand his operation the way he did.

"You have to have a system, a process, for everything," he said.

Pointing to the computer on the desk, "That thing should tell you how and when you need to do things, but you need to tell the computer when that stuff needs to be done. That's where your system starts."

Pretty amazing coming from a guy who could barely type and send an email. I had already come to this conclusion while sitting in the hospital bed, but the universe was clearly trying to tell me something. It was long past time to set up a system and start working smarter.

Worthless people live only to eat and drink; people of worth eat and drink only to live.

- Socrates

Establishing a Clear Vision for the Future

It wasn't long after my meetings with my mother and father that I realized how directionless my business had become. I had such lofty plans in the beginning. Not just for my business, but for me. "What happened?" I asked myself. I could only wonder. How did my business, and my life, get so far off track? The answer isn't as glorious as one might think.

The reason I got caught up in the operational-doldrums of my rental business is because it was so easy to do. I somehow confused having a good work ethic and 'working hard' with actually doing all the work myself. To add to that, I never placed any value on my free time. When a task came up that needed to be done, no matter how much or how little the cost, I simply did it myself. Over and over and over. Whether it was doing a bank reconciliation, placing an ad in the newspaper, fixing a furnace, or plunging a toilet, it was easy to do because I knew I had the ability to do it. Little by little, it all chips away at your Time-Wealth, and you'll never even notice it until you're laying in a hospital bed.

There is a reason you're in this business. If you haven't bought a rental property yet, there's a reason why you want in. The problem is that too often investors lose sight of this reason once they've accumulated a few properties and the nonsense and daily grind sets in. You need clarity as to why you want to buy rental properties and manage them yourself in the first place.

I'm not suggesting that buying rental properties and self-managing is a bad idea. After all, it has given me the ability to be a member of the Time-Wealthy and to enjoy the lifestyle I currently have. But when things go sideways in your business – and they will from time to time – you'll need to reference something more concrete than just "I want to make more money," or "being financially independent." As Steven Covey taught us in *The 7 Habits of Highly Effective People,* we need to begin with the end in mind. In a moment of frustration, you need a solid answer to the question, "Remind me again... why did I buy a rental property?" Otherwise, you'll wind up like the Jacksons, the old couple with the 25 rental units: defeated and bitter, with hardly any quality of life.

Know Your Why

I find that even successful people struggle to answer the question, "What are your goals?" This is something I became aware of as a manager when speaking to my employees during their evaluations.

I decided as part of the employee review process I would ask them to set goals, both personally and professionally, and to share them with me. By writing them down and knowing their goals, I felt I could hold them accountable when necessary, and get them to where they wanted to be much faster. What I discovered is that it is much more difficult for people to come up with goals than I realized. Tim Ferriss' book, *The 4 Hour Workweek* helped me develop a unique approach to goalsetting that I use whenever I help someone create a clear vision for their future. In this case, it was my employees.

Instead of the nebulous, "I want more money" answer to the goalsetting question, my approach often brought us both to a much deeper understanding of what was important to them and what they really wanted to achieve. More often than not, their goals usually had less to do with getting more money, and more to do with being challenged, having enriching experiences, and enjoying a better quality of life.

The approach I identified is to get to know my "Why?" Said another way, your "Why?" is the reason you'd get out of bed at 3 AM on a rainy Sunday. Not because you had to, but because you were so excited and eager to do it, you likely woke up before your alarm and jumped right up, ready to start the day.

In *The 4 Hour Workweek* the author brings us to a place where he reveals how pointless it is to base your goals around the question "What makes you happy?" Happiness is simply too vague, and I agree. Instead, we should be seeking the answer to a question much more specific and thorough. Rather than asking,

"What makes you happy?" he suggests you ask instead, "What excites you?" This is a great way to frame your thinking to get you the clarity you need for your vision.

Tremendous power comes with clarity. It's also incredibly liberating. The trouble is, it's not always easy to come up with an answer to "What excites you?" let alone figuring out what it is you really want. To help get your juices flowing in the proper context, consider thinking in terms of "Anticipated Joy".

Anticipated Joy

To help answer the question of "What excites you?" think of a time when you were looking forward to doing something and the anticipation was almost unbearable. Perhaps you recall the countdown leading up to a vacation you'd been planning, or the hours before a dinner-date with a special someone. Do you remember that feeling of anticipated joy? The tingle in your hands and butterflies in your stomach that made you feel almost giddy? This is the excitement you should be looking to replicate.

That excitement, that feeling of Anticipated Joy can help you uncover your "Why?" Figure out what excites you, find the things that cause you to experience Anticipated Joy, and you've found things worth pursuing. It's those things that would get you out of bed at 3 AM on a rainy Sunday.

In the context of goalsetting, this can be a state of "Being" (i.e. "Be" a college graduate), something around "Doing" (i.e. go on a month-long vacation to Belize), or something involved with "Having" (i.e. a motorcycle, boat, or perhaps a beach house with no mortgage). Whatever it is, your goal should scare you, perhaps even terrify you. That emotional response is not only good, it's necessary to ensure your goal doesn't get buried among all the little rocks and sand that fills your shoes from the daily minutia of operations. There will always be distractions diverting your attention from what you want, especially when things get difficult. However, once you know what matters to you most, once your vision is clear, you're much less likely to let things of little consequence distract you.

> **My favorite things in life don't cost any money. It's really clear that the most precious resource we all have is time.**
>
> **- Steve Jobs, Co-founder of Apple Computers**

The Tremendous Power of Clarity

I realize this section has nothing specifically to do with real estate. However, for you to be among the Time-Wealthy and create the life you want, it will be critical for you to free your time from the irrelevant and unimportant tasks that waste your day. Rediscovering time that was once wasted on nonsense can then be used to move you closer to your vision for the future.

Understanding what creates Anticipated Joy for you is a good first step to creating a solid vision. Take the time and get absolutely clear on what you want your future to look like. Your vision should be so clear that it is as obvious as the past. Once you can do that, write it down. Rewrite it every morning when you wake up, and right before you go to sleep. Keep it with you in your pocket and take it everywhere you go. Being clear in your vision is essential to ensure you use your Time-Wealth to create the world you want to live in. Otherwise, the sudden overabundance of unbridled and purposeless free time becomes a new problem.

Boredom, and a life without purpose, being the symptoms of an entirely different disease.

"There is tremendous power in clarity... Your vision should be so clear that it is as obvious as the past."

Having a bunch of real estate generating thousands of dollars of cash flow is a pretty cool thing. Spending all your time making it happen, on the other hand, is not. This is the fundamental difference between those that are Time-Weary, and those that are Time-Wealthy. The problem, is the group of the former often doesn't know there *is* a problem. They are simply too busy to notice how Time-Weary they really are, and life continues to pass them by.

Regardless of what we tell the world, or what we tell ourselves, our calendars reflect the things we are truly intentional about. If you want an accurate depiction of what it is you truly value, and what you actually spend your time doing, nothing is more brutally honest than the calendar. It not only reveals the people, things, and activities that were important to us yesterday, but who and what will be important to us tomorrow.

Stop and Consider:

> It's important you get your Vision so ingrained in you it becomes part of your daily activity. Get a stack of 3x5 index cards, write your Vision on it every morning as soon as you wake up, and again right before you go to sleep. The act of writing it over and over is critical. Be sure to use a new card each day.

Chapter Five

The Vision-Infrastructure-Process (VIP) Business Model

The mind, once stretched by a new idea, never returns to its original dimensions.

- Ralph Waldo Emerson

After my moment of clarity from the conversation with my mentor, and still marinating in my near-death experience in the hospital, I realized I had a serious problem of infrastructure and process. I didn't really start to face that problem until my three-day, $15,000 hospital stay forced it. The solution to this problem, I concluded, was going to require me to think and act in a completely different way. While I'm certainly no genius, I also knew I wasn't a complete dumbass either. I needed to come up with a system to free me from this raging barn fire I had created for myself. While gaining a clear vision for my future, I began to look towards the what else it would take to get me there.

The Vision-Infrastructure-Process Paradigm

Reflecting on the mess I was in, I came to realize that managing rental properties - whether you're a landlord or a property manager - is not about managing a piece of dirt or a house or a building. Let's face it, a building by itself doesn't pay the bills. It takes people, tenants, to do that. From a purely practical standpoint, managing rentals is really more about "people management" than it is about "property management".

As stated in the introduction, the Vision-Infrastructure-Process (VIP) Paradigm helps align everything in your business directed toward one central them – your Vision for the future. Remember, there is tremendous power in clarity, so be specific in terms of what you want. Starting with Vision will align everything else you construct in your business.

Process – The Whole Story

If you think of Infrastructure as the "train tracks" of your business, think of Process as the locomotive. The Process "locomotive" is powerful, and runs all the systems, processes, and rules upon which you'll operate. However, that's not the whole story behind Process.

Process, being the powerful locomotive it is, pulls two additional cars named Expectations and Behavior. I refer to this as the PEB Behavioral Model.

The Process-Expectations-Behavior (PEB) Model is designed to get results from people so they are satisfied, and you are successful. In order to elicit the behavior you want from people, they first have to be educated about your business process and know what is expected of them. Once you're sure they know the process and the expectations, *only then* can you hope to adjust someone's behavior. Trying to change someone's behavior without ensuring they first understand the process and expectations is often as aggravating for you as it is frustrating for them. If you hope to manage anyone effectively, you must consider these three things, specifically in this order: process, expectations, behavior.

Consider this example:

You're the boss, and you hire a new employee to come work for you. The first day after the interview, he shows up late. You ask him, "Why are you late?" to which he replies, "I'm not!" Not a good start.

You explain to your new hire that he wasn't clocked in on time and that is considered late. Your new hire looks at you puzzled, "I don't know how to clock in or even where the timeclock is!" Suddenly, you realize you should teach your new person the process.

You walk your new hire through the building, pointing out where he can park his car, where to put his personal items, and where the bathrooms are located. And, oh yeah, where the timeclock is and how to use it. You go through all the basics of the process. Thinking you're good, you send your new hire off to see him the next day.

The next day comes and unbelievably, he is late again! Exasperated, you're wondering if this has all been a mistake. This time, he clocked in 5 minutes late. You go back to your new hire and tell him, "You're late! You clocked in 5 minutes after you were supposed to be here. What is going on?"

Frustrated and embarrassed, your new hire is clearly upset. "What are you talking about? I clocked in right at 8 o'clock when my shift starts, just like you showed me yesterday!"

Yesterday you spent the entire morning teaching him the process, but you now realize that you never laid out the expectations. This is a "you" problem and not a problem of the new hire. "I'm sorry, you're right." You say slowly. "The expectation is that you're at your station at 8 o'clock, and that you're clocked in no later than 7:55 but no earlier than 7:50. That gives you ample time to get to where you need to be."

Now that you have outlined the process and the expectation, *only then* could you hope to adjust his behavior. If the new hire came in late yet again, you'd only need to make sure you review the process and expectations with him. Then, and only then, could you reasonably get him to change his behavior, addressing it accordingly.

It is with the PEB behavioral model that we will approach the management of the people-side of your rental business. Once you have a solid process in place, you will lay out the Expectations portion of this paradigm in your Lease Agreement, online FAQ, and SOP (Standard Operating Procedure). The Lease Agreement, FAQ, and SOP will refer back to the Process you have in place. If the resident doesn't perform the way you're wanting, say, for example they didn't pay the rent on time, it's at that point you make sure they understand the Rent-Paying Process (mail it, pay it on your website, etc.). After reviewing the Expectations as outlined in the Lease Agreement (rent is due by the 5th), you can then address the Behavior.

A New Jack

Remember our guy Jack? Let's look at how his life might look if he had implemented the Vision-Infrastructure-Process model for his real estate business. This time, it's Saturday morning and he's loading his golf bags into his friend's SUV. Jack wasn't much of a drinker, especially at 7:30 AM, but he was considering a celebratory toast with his friends once he got to the golf course.

Before leaving the house, Jack got an email notification from his new helper, a Virtual Assistant (VA) named Sarah. She had compiled a list of all the emergency calls from overnight, of which there were two. One tenant had a broken refrigerator, but a repairman had already been contacted by the VA and was scheduled to show up at the resident's house that morning. The other call was not an emergency at all. Rather, it was a resident who worked third shift calling to schedule a time to renew his lease. The VA already sent the lease via email, with a small increase in rent built in, to be signed by electronic signature. All was right in the world.

Do you see the striking difference between the two Jacks? It's obvious one is completely overwhelmed and losing control, and the other, although less directly involved, has everything completely under control. The new Jack understands that if he doesn't put a value on his free time, someone else will. The difference is infrastructure. The difference is the process. No longer Time-Weary, Jack is on the path to being a Time-Wealthy Investor.

Chapter Six

The Train and the Rails

The difference between a good business and a bad business is that good businesses throw up one easy decision after another. The bad businesses throw up painful decisions time after time.

- Charlie Munger

Considering how much effort investors put into so many other areas in their business, it makes no sense to me how little attention they pay to the framework upon which it will operate. I'd say it surprises me, but it doesn't. That's why my meeting with the Jacksons went absolutely nowhere. They didn't see value in infrastructure, so they saw no value in what I brought to the table.

Having a dearth of infrastructure is hardly a problem unique to the Jacksons though. Time after time, property investors buy real estate with little consideration as to how it will be managed after they close. Even though all the metrics have been carefully scrutinized, very little thought is given to exactly how those metrics will actually be achieved. Instead of a license to print money, it's a recipe for disaster.

In order for us to develop a process to manage a property effectively, you first have to realize you're in a "people" business. More specifically, you're in a service business. To effectively service customers, it's best to establish a process built on solid infrastructure in which to consistently handle them. Consistency, before anything else, should be your product. The only way to achieve that is with a sound process built on a solid infrastructure.

> *"Consistency, before anything else, should be your product. The only way to achieve that is with a sound process built on a solid infrastructure."*

Think about one of your favorite service businesses. Why is it your favorite? Is it because of the way they treat you when you come in? How do you feel when you leave? If you think about it, it's quite likely your favorite because you always have a consistent experience. Not because of how friendly or courteous the staff is, or the fact that they remember how you like your latte or your bacon and eggs, but because your experience of their product or service is always consistent. They use the same recipe over and over whether it's making soup or hiring employees. Any business that struggles with consistency struggles with everything else.

> Stop and Consider: Think of your favorite restaurant and a meal that you always enjoy. Your spouse calls to tell you you're going there tonight. Awesome! You anticipate your visit all day as the thought of savoring your favorite entrée fills your head. You arrive at the restaurant where you are promptly greeted by name and brought to your usual table. A few minutes later you order, the anticipation building within you as the smell of all the food around you reminds you of how hungry you are. You can hardly stand it! Not much later your meal is delivered to the table. Presented in its usual fashion,

the waiter asks if you would like anything else. You politely decline, trying not to be rude as you have finally arrived at the moment you've been anticipating all day. With little delay, utensils in hand, you place that first decadent forkful in your mouth…

Only to find out, that night, the chef changed the recipe.

Epic fail.

Was the meal bad? Maybe not, but that's not the problem. The real problem is the expectation of your experience was altered and you were given no choice in the matter. It's as if someone placed a blindfold on you, told you they are going to feed you a strawberry, and instead gave you a green bean. You might like green beans, but you were expecting a strawberry.

From the customer's perspective, there is considerable stress involved if there is inconsistency between what they are told and what they receive. Inconsistency violates the trust the customer has placed in you, the service provider. The business has lost credibility, and in the service industry, credibility is currency. People must trust you and have to believe you are credible. They trust you to deliver on your implied promise to simply do what you say you will.

"Any business that struggles with consistency struggles with everything else."

Consistency should be your product. Your process must be simple enough to be universally applied. Every single time one of your customers has an interaction, they should experience the same level of consistency no matter who they talk to or when they come in.

A Day in the Life of a Landlord

In setting up the infrastructure for your real estate business, consider all the tasks that need to be performed. Just by the very nature of this business, the landlord wears many different hats. Many of the individual tasks and roles are not only interrelated, but have a direct impact on one another. For example, you might have a reliable and consistent mechanism for collections, but having an inconsistent maintenance function can render your collection process completely impotent. The argument goes something like, "Well, my landlord doesn't want to fix anything, so I'm not paying rent!"

Consider for a moment a day in the life of a typical landlord, and all the tasks they do. From the very beginning the landlord is the one who places the ads in the paper or online and answers the phone and all the questions that follow. It's the landlord who conducts the showing at the property, where everyone is smiling and getting along. It's the landlord who conveys promises such as: "We plan to paint," along with "I'll also replace the carpet in the living room before you move in."

It's the landlord who then works through the application process, followed by the lease signing, then the move-in. The few promised maintenance items were taken care of by the landlord, who is also the maintenance technician. Everything is going great, that is, until the first month's rent comes due.

Now the collection agent is needed, a duty also performed by the landlord. Here's where things can easily go off the rails. In the mind of the tenant, the landlord, up to this point, has acted as the "Good Guy" in the capacity of the leasing agent and maintenance technician, only to become the "Bad Guy" as the collection agent. Even if this emotional switching of gears is not difficult for you, it is extremely difficult for the residents. They will even say ridiculous things like:

"Yeah, our landlord is a great guy until he wants his money...."

This is usually the part where banging your head on a curb feels better than trying to understand this type of logic.

Let's face it though, even if **you** can switch gears from one role to the next without too much thought, it's simply exhausting to do so. Imagine being at work performing some high-level task, or at your daughter's dance recital, and your resident calls to complain about a late fee. This is why the private landlord who has no infrastructure or solid process will struggle when compared to one who does.

Consider for a moment if you did nothing else but put in place some tools and establish a well-defined process for rent collection. By defining the process well, and making it very clear, this task can easily be delegated to someone else. This would save a ton of headaches for you and make the rent collection process easy for your residents to understand. In other words, a well-defined collections process establishes a measure of consistency for your customers.

I'm not suggesting you run out and hire someone right away to do your collections, or any other function for that matter. Don't confuse having an employee or an outsourced company for having infrastructure or a process. You must clearly define things first before delegating any function to someone else. Whichever function we're talking about, get the process established and up and running smoothly and work out all the kinks before you have someone else perform it. Simply having someone else take over your mess will not improve the order of the universe. Remember that a well-defined process running on sound infrastructure creates consistency, and that's what we're looking for.

Back to Jack

Let's go back about six months. Jack was just starting to realize he needed to change the way he did business. Jack's home office was in shambles, his entire Saturday consumed by aggravating conversations and frustrating circumstances. It was now a little after 6PM, and his wife was going to be knocking on the door to his home office any time now. A few minutes later, she appeared in the doorway.

"Sweetheart?" She called out to him in a tender voice.

Jack looked up at his wife and smiled. In her hands, she had two drinks from Starbucks.

"I'll take the one with the poison," he joked, frustrated from his experience from the day.

Jack's wife smiled and walked into the room. She slid some papers to the side and carefully set his drink down on the desk.

"How did it go today?" She asked gently, sensing his frustration.

Jack didn't say anything. He sighed and shook his head slightly.

Jack's wife stood next to him for a moment, looking at her husband who was feeling defeated. Smiling, she placed a hand on his shoulder, squeezing gently to let him know she understood. She turned and leaned against his desk, staring intently at her drink.

"You know what's amazing about Starbucks?" she started, "No matter how many times I go there, they always get my drink just how I want it." Her cup rested against her chin. "Kind of amazing when you think about it."

Jack stared at his drink as well; he was too mentally exhausted to do much else. He appreciated his wife going and getting Starbucks for him. He was fascinated by their operation – and his wife was right – no matter how many times they buy drinks there, Starbucks is incredibly consistent.

"Why do you think that is?" Jack asked his wife. "What do you think is their secret behind their consistency, behind it all for that matter?"

Jack's wife sipped her drink, looking off, as if staring at something in the distance.

"It's a machine. No matter which one you go to, they are all basically the same," she said. "Sure, the layout from one to the next is a little different, but I'm sure it's the same computer system, the same equipment, even the way they train their employees to make coffee is the same no matter which one you go to."

There was a message in her words, whether she realized it or not, and Jack was very ready to listen. He'd been run by his rental business for far too long and for the first time he realized that he really didn't have a business. He really had nothing that actually resembled a rental business except a collection of properties. He started thinking about all the things he needed to put in place so his business looked more like a business. Perking up, he felt some energy returning to his body.

"Thanks for the coffee sweetheart," Jack said. "Let's go to dinner, but I want to stop somewhere first."

As to methods, there may be a million and then some, but principles are few. The man who grasps principles can successfully select his own methods. The man who tries methods, ignoring principles, is sure to have trouble.

- Harrington Emerson

Laying the Groundwork

There is a considerable difference between infrastructure and process, although up until now it may seem as if I were using those terms interchangeably. Remember the analogy introduced earlier, where the train tracks are the infrastructure and a locomotive is the process. The more solid and well-laid the tracks (infrastructure), the faster and smoother the train (process) can run. Having a solid infrastructure is key to properly running the Process-Expectations-Behavior (PEB) model.

The rest of this book is broken up into four parts. We've already covered Vision and why that is important, the remaining parts will cover the rest of the VIP Paradigm. Infrastructure will take up much of Part One. Part Two will introduce you to Process. The remaining Parts, Three and Four, will dig much deeper into the last two parts of the PEB Behavioral Model – Expectations and Behavior respectively. Each of these parts will build on one another to set up your real estate business.

Part One will deal specifically with the basics of infrastructure you will need, or should at least consider, to design and organize your business framework upon which everything will operate.   From purchasing powerful software, to assembling an A-list of players for your team, you will learn the basics of how to manage risk and how it can be done – all at minimal cost. By starting off with infrastructure, you will be able to more easily define your process for a given task. Processes developed in the context of your infrastructure are more likely to run smoothly and be consistently applied. Most importantly, you will much more likely establish processes that work well, are cohesive, and don't contradict one another.

Part Two introduces the specifics of the Process in the PEB model, where you build the dynamic engine which will run on the tracks you built in Part One. This section will give you much-needed context to put Part One in perspective and understand what it's all for. As you develop your processes for various functions, you sometimes need to go back and develop your infrastructure further so your process runs more efficiently and effectively. Don't get discouraged, when it comes to Process and Infrastructure, work on them like a sudoku puzzle. Figure out the parts you're able to, then add to the other parts when it makes sense. Don't become paralyzed by thinking one part needs to be set up before another is implemented.

Part Three will cover Expectations and how you convey them to your residents. Much of this is passed on through your lease, but other methods involve using an online FAQ (Frequently Asked Questions) and SOP (Standard Operating Procedure). For those of you with rental properties, this section allows you to align your infrastructure, processes, and risk tolerance with what you're currently doing and all the tips you've learned along the way. If you're starting fresh, you get to set your expectations from the perspective of someone who has been down the road before you.

Part Four, the Behavior portion of the PEB Model, encourages the behavior you want and discourages the behavior you don't. This addresses **your** behavior just as much as it addresses that of your residents. From learning about the Drama Triangle and how to stay out of it, to the fundamentals of negotiations, it's all there.

In the chapters that follow, each element will be discussed in significant detail. As mentioned earlier, set these things up as you **need** them, not as you **read** them. As you're reading, if you start to get overwhelmed with where to start, find the one or two items keeping you up at night and work from the items you know you need the most. This is where having an absolutely clear vision is not only helpful, but necessary to avoid becoming an emotional train wreck.*

It excites me knowing you are being armed with the tools for you to take charge of your life and your business. Soon, you will be living life on your terms, doing all the things that excite you, and creating the life you want.

Stop and Consider: For clarification purposes, there are two models at work here. The Vision-Infrastructure-Process (VIP) Paradigm is the business model – it is the roadmap as to how you will set up your business. The Process-Expectations-Behavior (PEB) Model is simply the "Process" portion of the VIP Paradigm further defined and explained in how it can be applied day-to-day.

*If you still need help getting clarity with your Vision, don't despair. More resources are readily available at www.LandlordCoach.com/twiBook.

One Final Thought on Vision

Before you move on to the more technical parts of this book, and the remaining parts of the VIP Paradigm, stop, be present for a moment. Quiet your mind. Consider what you would do if you had all the cash flow you needed and didn't worry about income production.

What would your World look like? What would you create?

That's your Vision.

Now, let's put an Infrastructure in place that's in alignment with that Vision.

Part I - Infrastructure

Chapter Seven

Property Management Software

The software is where the magic is. If you're going to have all this power, be simple enough, appealing enough and cool enough, it's going to be because the software was right.

- Bill Gates

Property Management (PM) software is on the top of the infrastructure list for a variety of reasons. Many of the other infrastructure and process items we discuss later will reference the PM software in one way or another. Fortunately, there are numerous Property Management Software systems to choose from. I don't want to get into a classification discussion as to whether I feel one is particularly "Good" or "Bad". My litmus test for PM software is simple: the software must be customizable so that *I tell it how to run my business, not the other way around.*

I know some of you will be hesitant to adopt PM software, but no matter how complex or sophisticated your spreadsheets are in Excel, they will be nothing compared to the capability of good PM software. Trust me, the time-dividends alone will make it all worth it. Besides, we're building a business here. Build your business on a system that is scalable and one that someone else can operate so you don't have to.

Customization

Many software providers claim to be customizable but they really aren't, at least not to the point you'll need them to be. Some will allow you to charge late fees only in a certain way, for example. The problem is, you might have to kiss one or two frogs before you find your Prince.

I decided to go with a more customizable Property Management software because I wanted to stand out from other companies which were simply using the popular and well-marketed software. After looking at all of my choices, I decided that PropertyBoss, albeit more expensive than the other options, was best suited to my operation. http://propertyboss.com/ For those of you that have operations consisting of 20 units and up, you might consider this software as an option. Another good option which I felt had a similar layout is PropertyWare which you can find at www.propertyware.com.

A different option is the software offered by National Tenant Network, which they provide for free to their customers who utilize their Resident Screening service. Visit the site www.ntnonline.com for additional information. If you plan on expanding your operation, at a certain point you may need to replace this infrastructure with something more permanent, such as PropertyBoss or PropertyWare.

> Note: These are only several recommendations out of many others in the PM Software industry. Since the first printing of this book, roughly a dozen software providers have become relevant in this arena. These software products will continue to evolve and new players will

enter the market, so be sure to look beyond the ones I've mentioned here for the product that serves you best.

Here is a list of the basics you should expect from your Property Management software. Get familiar with them now, and be sure to come back to them when you're ready to start shopping providers:

- Resident Database – Your system should keep track of all your resident information: contact phone numbers and emails, Social Security numbers, bank account and credit card numbers, emergency contact information, plus any notes you'd like to keep on your residents (such as they work 3rd shift, they prefer to be contacted by text message, or that they don't like the smell of bananas).

  Your database must be able to perform a search, or sort, by property address or resident name. This is important because as you expand, you might remember the address of the property but not the person's name, or vice versa. This will also enable you to move back and forth between accounts faster and not zap your brain power needed for other things. In addition to residents' contact information, you must also have the ability to track their payment history plus any notes of client interactions. This is incredibly important for documenting phone calls (inbound and outbound) as well as face to face interactions.

- Rent Receivable – Even the most basic PM software will have a tenant register showing you a history of what's been charged and when rent has been paid. Beyond that, it must help you keep track of who owes you money without having to go into each individual register. Even if you have a small operation, this is absolutely paramount. Timely receipt of rent revenue is critical to a sound operation. If you lose track of who owes you money, you'll bleed to death as expenses pile up with no income to offset them. Collection of receivables is one of the critical areas in which landlords fail.

- Bookkeeping – You should be able to track revenues and expenses for each property as well as each unit for multi-family properties. If a repair or utility bill, for example, needs to be charged to the resident, it's often as easy as checking a box or quickly flipping over to another register. This is also helpful in keeping track of which units are your top performers and which are your dogs.

- Lease Status – Lease Status reflects if the lease is current, expiring, or month to month. You should be able to keep track of lease status either by simply running a report or having the software alert you automatically. This is extremely important so you can always ensure you're staying ahead of the game and always negotiating from a position of strength.

- Maintenance Requests – You should be able to keep track of maintenance requests including when they were called in, who the repair was assigned to, when the work order was closed out, and what was the outcome. This will be extremely important when you're working with a particularly difficult resident who claims to have notified you of maintenance needs, which incidentally, nearly always coincides with the reason their rent is late. Most online systems have the capability for residents to enter their own maintenance requests, as well as generate a unique Work Order Number or Tracking Number that the resident can reference. This not only holds you accountable, but it almost eliminates the "I called and told you about this maintenance issue three times" argument. If they don't have a work order number to reference, or it's not in our system, it's safe to say we were never informed. This feature alone is enough to keep you sane and in control.

> Stop and Consider: I can't tell you how many maintenance issues residents swore they told me about that I honestly did not remember during my cell-phone-only and pre-Property-Management-software days. Wanting to give people the benefit of the doubt, I ended up waiving far too many late fees and making rent concessions for not addressing their maintenance concerns. It was absolutely maddening, and it was costing me a ton of money. Be careful here, and remember, this is a customer service business. Don't use this tool as a weapon to beat them with. This isn't about being right; it is about addressing their maintenance issues.

- File System – You should be able to upload and maintain an organized file system. Having the ability to look at a scanned copy of someone's lease electronically is so much easier than having to spend time filing paperwork and then retrieving it later. Scanning and uploading such documents, as well as their renter's insurance policy, property inspection reports, and similar documents, saves time and eliminates the aggravation of having to track down their hard-copy equivalents. Just check to be sure that copies of such documents would suffice in court, should you ever have to file for eviction or for a judgement. You will also be able to do this at the property-level for documents such as mortgages, property tax records, Home Owners Association (HOA) documents and correspondence, insurance documents, warranty information on appliances and so forth.

- Advertising Photos – This is a way to store marketing photos you can use over and over for advertising from one leasing season to the next. Unless there were major changes to the property, these can be used for several years without needing to be updated. Reusing these photos saves a tremendous amount of time when you're needing to find a new renter.

Remember, all Property Management software systems are not equal, so the one you're looking at may offer more features and functionality, but certainly should not provide less. Once you start researching PM software providers, insist you get an online demonstration along with a trial version to play around with for at least 30 days so you can make an informed decision. Here's a list of questions for you to narrow the field:

- Does this software operate in the cloud? Most PM software does, and in fact, you will want it to. Later on, when we talk about using Virtual Assistants, you don't want to have to worry about your VA's ability to access the PM software. Just be sure your internet connection can handle the interface without a lag or an annoying delay, which can be a giant pain. Unless you live in a very remote area with spotty internet, I would suggest this option.

- If the software does not operate in the cloud, or you're choosing to run the software on your computer, do you have to pay for updates? What kind of support can you expect if you buy the software? Can you install it on multiple computers? Keep in mind that updates may be critical. If you're using non-updated software, the software provider may not provide technical support to you. Be sure to find this out in advance, and if you plan to install it on multiple computers, be certain you know the cost.

- Does this software interface with your accounting software, such as QuickBooks? If not, will your CPA be able to easily compile the necessary data for your tax returns and financial statements? This is CRUCIAL to operating your business. Without an accounting function, you don't have a business. DO NOT DISCOUNT THIS IMPORTANT FEATURE! Work with your accountant to make sure that this PM software will provide the data needed to make informed choices and prepare your taxes without a lot of hoop-jumping at the end of the year.

- Can this software integrate with your website? Even if you don't have a website yet, you need to plan for this now. This feature is vitally important for marketing your vacant units in real-time so you don't have to hassle with remembering to go online to post them. Can you create an online application for prospects to fill out? Can your residents submit maintenance work orders through a resident portal on your website as well as make online payments? Features such as these will save you a tremendous amount of time, and will make your life markedly easier when it comes to processing resident applications, performing rent collection, and the overall management of your resident's needs.

- What type of training and support do they offer? Most people only learn about 30% of a software's capabilities, enough to support their daily operations and that's about it. To get the most out of your PM software, training should be intentional. This is especially true as PM software systems evolve and are enhanced, or when hiring employees or Virtual Assistants. Be aware that some providers will offer training for free, and others may charge you for it beyond the basics. Make sure you know the costs up front.

- Across Property Management software providers, most of the basic functions are the same. That is, they all have resident portals and other portals for different customers and vendors to log into. The more you shop around, the more you'll see this to be the case. Consider what this portal looks like from your client's perspective. You should be able to utilize it as a resident so you can see how easy is it to use and what their experience will be when they use it.

- Can you email residents directly from your system for rent collection purposes or to follow up with work orders? Are there any automated emails you could set up to be sent to your residents a few days prior to rent being due? This is an important time-saver so you can make sure things are managed without having to do them manually each month.

- Is a contract required? I'd be very skeptical of providers who want to lock you into long-term contracts. PM software providers realize it's a pain in the neck to switch once you've been a customer for a while, and the contract is just another way to control you.

> Stop and Consider: DO NOT BUY THE FIRST PM SOFTWARE YOU TRY! Some of them are particularly good at marketing their own software with salesmen that will NEVER leave you alone even after you've told them you've chosen another provider. After the initial

good-impression and cleverness wears off, you need to have good PM software on which to build your processes. Take the time to vet them as best you can so you don't wind up with software from a company that was only good at marketing their product and not much else.

Selecting a good Property Management software begins to set up the bones of your business architecture. **Don't discount this and don't rush it.** Remember, in the beginning you don't know what you don't know. Take the time to educate yourself and don't be bullied by aggressive PM software salespeople. Take full advantage of trial periods, and be sure you start the trial when you have enough time in your calendar to fully test drive it. I highly recommend you compare two or three different providers before making a decision. Try each out for a month, one at a time. Get the overall sense of what you like and what will work best for you.

Infrastructure

Chapter Eight

Accounting

If you don't have accounting,

you don't have a business.

> **- Marcus Lemonis, T.V.
> Show "The Profit"**

This book is about identifying at the outset that rental properties are, at their core, small businesses. They are not what I would refer to as an investment in the purest sense. You have assets and liabilities, revenues and expenses, customers and vendors. To any first-year accounting student, that is a business.

I know, I know, your eyes are probably already glazing over at the mere sight of the word "accounting" but let's face it, every business must have an accounting function. Without an accounting function, you simply don't have a business; you have a hobby. My intent here is not to transform you into an accountant. I do however, want to educate you as to what good accounting software will do for you and why you need it.

Accounting Software

I've never been particularly impressed with the accounting data most property management software systems provide, but I'd let your CPA be the judge. If you are going to choose accounting software, I think the best accounting data providers are the ones specializing in that field, such as QuickBooks, Xero, or Peachtree (now known as Sage 50). My preference and experience is with QuickBooks, which is one of the main reasons why I like PropertyBoss because they integrate so well. The developers at PropertyBoss realized that QuickBooks is good at accounting, so they didn't attempt to reinvent the wheel when it came to the accounting function.

Of the accounting software choices I mentioned, QuickBooks seems to be far and away the clear choice for most of the CPAs I've talked to. It's what most bankers and other professionals in the financial industry have come to know as well. For the few hundred dollars you spend, you get a very robust program with excellent reporting features that would take hours to replicate by hand.

This will take you a little bit of time to set up, which the QuickBooks set-up wizard walks you through step by step. It will ask you about your business, if you have employees, what assets you own for your business, what liabilities you have, and so forth. It will also help you set up what is known as your "Chart of Accounts". Think of your Chart of Accounts as a list of the categories for all your revenues (money coming in) and expenses (money going out), in addition to what you own in the name of your business (houses, appliances, etc.) and what you owe (mortgages, credit card debt, and other debts). However, before you get too far down the road, I STRONGLY recommend that you don't set up your Chart of Accounts without the assistance of your accountant. If you don't have a CPA already, we'll discuss how to find and select one at the end of the chapter.

If you already have a Chart of Accounts set up and in use, that's fine. I still suggest having an accountant review it so you are getting the best data to support good financial decision making. If you lack good financial data, it's like driving a speedboat in the fog. Exciting maybe, but foolish and most certainly dangerous!

> Stop and Consider: You shouldn't view your accounting function as a "necessary evil" or simply a cost of doing business. It's as important as buying an updated map before a long journey. It will tell you all the sights to look for along the way, as opposed to just "heading west". I would argue that it might be fun to go exploring in life, but don't do it in business. If you want to be among the best, you have to do what the best are doing. Setting budgets, tracking metrics, monitoring revenues and expenses, and having a systematic process for reviewing financial data – that is what the best are doing.

One final thought on your accounting software. If your property management software includes an accounting function, show it to your CPA first to make sure it will provide the necessary information to produce solid financial statements without having to re-create them in another system. That can be incredibly time-consuming and redundant, and unnecessarily expensive if you're paying your accountant to compile those data.

Selecting an Accountant (CPA)

You have the very basics of a business in place, or at least you're considering your options. Now you need to hire a financial professional to help you focus on the right things in your growing business. Having a good financial person on your team is an absolute must. You can't hope to make sound business decisions, or even have any sense of direction, without a person like this in place. You can self-administer this for a while, but why would you want to? Your job is to be focused on the success and operation of your real estate business, not on keeping up with the tax laws and all the nuances of accounting.

> Stop and Consider: In his book, *Good to Great*, the author Jim Collins likens a business to a bus. The goal is to get the right people on the bus and in the right seats, not to mention booting the wrong people off the bus. From this perspective, get the right people on the bus as early as you can on your journey and ***stop trying to do everything on your own***. Your journey will be much more enjoyable if you're the navigator more often than the bus driver, the mechanic, AND the guy who fills it with gas – you will get to your destination much faster too.

I think at this point it's important to clarify something. When I use the word "accountant" I'm referring to a CPA, which is a Certified Public Accountant. A CPA is a licensed professional. Having one on your team will pay huge dividends in your financial future. A word of caution, just like any other business or professional, all CPAs are not created equal. This means that the CPA you're using, if you're already using one, may or may not be the right person for you. Many people incorrectly assume that since someone is a CPA, all they do is prepare tax returns. While this is true for many CPAs, their real value is being able to look at the financial data and determine what is going on with your business, where you're headed, and to what adjustments to make along the way.

Below is a list of questions you should consider when interviewing (or reconsidering) a CPA. Keep in mind that if you live in a small town, your choices might be limited, so be open to looking at the next town over or a larger city. I realize that firing your current CPA can be difficult, but this is YOUR business. You owe it to yourself and your family to make sure you have the best qualified professional to help you along the way. Most decisions like this are not difficult to determine. I will acknowledge they might be emotionally difficult to execute, but as the CEO of your enterprise it comes with the job description. Most CPAs, if they are true professionals, won't even think twice about it. Losing a client is just a temporary blip on the radar. Just tear off the bandage and move on.

I interviewed a few CPAs I know and they came up with several questions people should consider asking when selecting an accounting professional. The following is a list of their questions plus a few questions of my own:

- What experience do you have working with clients with rental properties?

  Consider both tax preparation and the accounting side of things in their answer. If they are more focused on agriculture and manufacturing, this might be a concern. It's important for you to feel comfortable that they are going to know and be aware of any changes to the tax laws concerning ownership of rental properties. **Ask them if they are familiar with the tax implications and tax planning of residential rental real estate.** Ask for specific examples and gauge them against the answers you get from the other CPAs you are interviewing.

- What services can you offer me? What kind of support should I expect from you?

  Your accountant should be able to outline the services and support they can offer. This is where a CPA should bring value far in excess of just preparing your tax returns. Consider things like QuickBooks training, setting up your chart of accounts, bookkeeping, budgeting, strategic business planning, tax planning, and consulting.

- What are your standard hourly charges for your various services? What kind of things should I expect to pay for?

  Make sure you are clear on this up front. Having an accounting professional on your team is incredibly important, but it shouldn't cause you to go broke either. Find out the circumstances for which you should expect to be charged, such as when you need to pick up the phone and ask a basic question or if they answer an email. Don't be offended if they charge you for things such as this. CPAs are constantly having people try to get in their heads and pick their brain for free. Be respectful of their time and knowledge, and they will appreciate you much more as a client. Keep in mind too, if they are preparing your taxes and you are getting a tax refund, the preparer's fee should **never** be based on a percentage of your refund. Also, your refund should **never** under any circumstances go into the preparer's bank account.

- Do you have a flat fee billing program whereby you are billed a flat fee each month for a certain number of hours of service, regardless of the service?

  This feature can even out your cash flow expenditures. Make sure you understand what this charge covers and what is extra.

- How technology savvy is your firm? Do you utilize online accounting programs, portals, and secure delivery transfer?

  Many accounting firms are storing their data in the cloud now. This will save you a tremendous amount of time from having to drop things off to your accountant's office, and will keep everything organized. Even if you're not particularly tech-savvy, these tools are extremely easy to use and will help keep you organized.

- What is your preferred form of communication – in person, email, or phone call? How soon do you respond to emails and my workload questions and needs?

  This is necessary to know up front, especially if you don't plan on visiting your CPA in person very often, or if you won't be available by phone during the work day. It's also helpful if you plan to employ a Virtual Assistant in the future knowing they can communicate with each other by email. As for responsiveness, I don't know that there is such a thing as an "Accounting Emergency". As long as my CPA responds within a day or two, I'm ok with it. If your expectation is much faster, make sure you tell them this up front so there's no disappointment in the future.

Some other considerations:

- Ask for two or three references of similar clients who you can talk to before deciding to hire them.

- Ask if their firm is "peer reviewed". This means that their accounting/bookkeeping practice is audited every three years by another external accounting firm. You can expect this from higher quality firms, and they should receive clean peer review reports.

- When searching for a CPA, one resource you can use is your state's CPA society membership directory. A list is available through the AICPA, at www.AICPA.org Here you can check the CPA's credentials, any history of any disciplinary action, and their license status.

- Make sure that your CPA is available year-round for any issues that might arise after the return is filed. This isn't a February-to-April job for a CPA if they are a true professional, so make sure that they aren't going to be in San Juan for five months when you're trying to plan a tax strategy meeting in the fall.

- **Never sign a blank tax form!** This request raises a red flag. This is a legal document, so make sure you go over it with your CPA. You should be able to take a copy of your return with you to review with someone else if you don't understand what your CPA is telling you.

- Consider how long they have been in business. This is especially important if you're dealing with a small firm of one CPA and an assistant. There's nothing inherently wrong with a small accounting firm as they can be more affordable than larger ones. You just need to consider that, as your business grows and evolves, they might not be the right person for you five years from now.

> Stop and Consider: By 2009, I hadn't filed my taxes for several years since everything for me financially was just a mess. I went with a one-

man CPA firm early on to save money and help get me on track. He did great to get my tax returns caught up and got me sorted out with the IRS. A few years later though, I realized that I needed to change to a different CPA to better suit my business needs. It wasn't a particularly difficult decision, but it did require a bit of an awkward conversation when I told my him I was going somewhere else.

Bottom line, you need to have a measure of comfort before you allow this person to root through all your financial statements and involve them in your business. Just like with your PM software provider, interview several before making your decision. Hire slowly, and if they turn out not to be what you thought, let them go quickly and move on.

Basics of Financial Statements

For those of you who understand financial statements already, you get to breeze through this section. It would be a waste of trees to devote the next five pages on all the particulars that could easily be expanded upon elsewhere for those that need it. For a quick and easy explanation of a Balance Sheet and Income Statement that is relevant to your real estate business, please visit www.LandlordCoach.com/twiBook.

Infrastructure

Chapter Nine

Automating Communications

Ultimate automation... will make our modern industry as primitive and outdated as the stone age man looks to us today.

- Albert Einstein

After I started with some basic infrastructure improvements, most notably putting the PM Software in place, I began thinking of ways I could automate some of the basic processes and routines I was already doing. In order to automate, I'd need to consider *what* exactly I could automate, plus the infrastructure I would need to help accomplish that.

I shifted my thinking and forced myself to stop and take a real accounting of where my time was being spent each day, looking for at least one thing I could automate. Surprisingly, it took me less than five minutes to figure out. The one thing that chewed up a tremendous amount of my day was talking on the phone. My cell phone was an enormous distraction for me. Specifically, the one area I could automate was getting information to prospects about my available rental units.

Every Thursday, I placed a call to advertise my available rental units in the classified ads section of the weekend newspaper for Friday, Saturday, and Sunday. This ad usually generated calls all weekend and throughout the week, as many people would buy the Sunday classifieds for their housing search. In addition to the ads, I also had yard signs out with my cell number on them. These two things in combination were remarkably effective in getting people to call me about what was available.

I noticed people almost always asked the same ten questions, or a variation of the following:

- Where is this house/apartment located?
- How much is the rent?
- How much is the security deposit?
- What utilities do I have to pay?
- Will you accept work in lieu of the security deposit?
- Can the security deposit be paid in installments?
- How much will it cost to move in?
- Do you accept pets, and if so, what kind?
- When is it available?
- What is your application process?

There were other questions here and there, but far and away these were the ones I was asked over and over and over. The really aggravating part was, even though much of this information was placed in the ad, people calling from the classifieds would still ask the same questions. On top of that, with very few exceptions, nearly every call took at least 15 minutes. Some calls went far longer when the caller felt the need to tell me all about their situation and how they were unjustly evicted because they had to pay for their cat's "whiskerectomy" or something similar. This added to my frustration when these calls came in while I was in the middle of doing something else. No matter if I was deep in the process of fixing something or doing a showing with a prospect, I would often get called by people who didn't use any form of punctuation in their sentences. Handling these calls was another unfortunate symptom of my poorly developed infrastructure.

Going Automated

With this issue identified, my first step towards automation was fairly easy. Starting with a simple phone system, I set about my first level of automation to help with all the responses I was getting to my advertising.

I knew a website would help with this problem, but I wanted a phone number people could call for information while they were out driving around or after-hours. I put in place an automated phone system called "Grasshopper" http://grasshopper.com/. Designed for people who had home offices, this system made the solo-entrepreneur sound like one of the big guys. It could be set-up to be answered by an auto-attendant, which is basically the voice that answers most calls for businesses with "Thank you for calling ABC Company. Press 1 for sales, press 2 for customer service…"

I figured out I could use the same system in a slightly different way that would allow me to save an enormous amount of time and provide my prospects a lot of valuable information. The Grasshopper system assigned me a virtual, toll-free phone number allowing me to set up an automated menu I could easily adjust based on my available units. It took me a few days to put together and tweak the script I wanted, but after recording the message for each available unit, my time-dividends were large and near-instantaneous.

With my toll-free number, people could now call and get automated information for the 10 most-asked questions about my available rental units – 24 hours a day, 7 days a week. I placed this number in all my advertising – print, online, and eventually on my website. My auto-attendant script went like this:

> "Hi, you've reached the 24-hour information line for June Palms. Please select from the following menu of options for our housing available for immediate occupancy:
>
> For the three-bedroom, two-bath house with fenced yard, located at 123 Main Street for $950 per month, please press 801.
>
> For the large two-bedroom duplex with washer/dryer hookups, located at 456 Elk Street for $750 per month, please press 802.
>
> For the ground floor two-bedroom apartment with dishwasher and washer/washer dryer installed, located at 789 Oak Street for $575 per month, please press 803.
>
> For the second-story, one-bedroom apartment with washer/dryer included, located at 1234 Cyprus Street for $475 per month, please press 804."

This was the main menu prospects would hear when they called. I will show you a sample script for one of the properties here in a moment, but first, I want to point out how everything scripted here was done with a purpose.

Notice how early in the script it was mentioned that these properties were available for immediate occupancy. I did this so people calling in April, for example, wouldn't waste their time (or mine) if they were looking for a place for November. That amount of lead time isn't normal in my market. Notice too that I listed these properties in order of price and not in order of bedrooms, bathrooms or other amenities. I want potential customers to listen to all my higher priced options first. It's an automated way to upsell without being pushy. The other benefit to doing this is that callers get to hear about all your available units instead of just the one they were calling about.

Notice too I listed some of the main elements I wanted to promote in the short listing. Of course, I will want to expand in more detail in my long listing description once they select their choice, but I want to give them one potato chip so they become interested in the whole bag. If I just said, "For the 3-bedroom house at 123 Main Street" they would not be all that excited about it. Adding the fact that it also has a second bathroom and a fenced yard could make all the difference to someone and it takes only a few seconds more effort.

No matter which unit I'm advertising, even for the lowest quality one I had, I always found something redeeming to promote. If you're struggling, consider some of the following ideas:

- Close to walking trails, parks, library, public transportation, downtown, Art District, etc.
- Cathedral ceilings, open floor plan, located on a quiet street
- Pet friendly, trash and water paid (for apartments typically), dog park nearby
- Off street parking, extra storage, bicycle storage

Stop and Consider: Be careful not to mention being close to churches or specific schools; even seemingly innocuous language such as "Family Friendly" can easily become a Fair Housing complaint. Most landlords unintentionally violate Fair Housing Laws through their advertising. While Fair Housing laws are beyond the scope of this book, I STRONGLY recommend you take a Fair Housing class so you don't unintentionally violate the law. Ignorance of the law will NOT protect you.

Don't assume that you know all the laws, and that means all of them – Federal, State and Local. Lawsuits are the latest form of lottery, and ignorance of the law could cost you dearly. Take the time to educate yourself, especially if you plan to be a full-time investor.

Once you have your main menu nailed down, you will need to develop a script for each individual property. This may sound time-consuming, especially if you have a lot of properties, but the effort you put in now is well worth the time-dividends later on. Plus, you can reuse the same script over and over by just changing a few things that are relevant to that specific property.

Referring back to the auto-attendant script the caller first hears, let's assume they pressed '801' and wanted to hear about the three-bedroom, two-bath home for $950 per month. Here is a sample script I would use for the individual property listing:

> "Thank you for calling about the three-bedroom, two-bath home for $950 per month. This single-family, ranch-style home is located at 123 Main Street and is available for immediate occupancy. Features include refrigerator, gas stove, central air, dishwasher, and washer-dryer. Other features include a fully-fenced back yard, off-street parking, an attached two-car garage with remotes, and a dry utility basement for storage.
>
> The rent for this home is $950 per month, and the security deposit is also $950. We require the first and last month's rent plus deposit to be paid prior to moving in. We may work out a different payment arrangement based on your credit application. The application fee is $25 per adult, and each adult residing in the home must be listed on the application. The resident is responsible for paying the gas, electric, and water utilities. Some

pets may be acceptable for a small additional monthly charge and $150 non-refundable pet fee.

If you're interested in viewing this home at 123 Main Street, please press zero to be connected to a member of the June Palms Staff during office hours. Or you may leave a name and number after the tone, and someone will call you back within one business day. To see photos and a floorplan, check out our website at June Palms dot com. [We will discuss websites in a later chapter.]

Thanks again for calling June Palms. Relax; we've got it!"

Notice how I touched on all 10 questions people frequently asked when calling me previously. For example, I reiterated that the house was available for immediate occupancy to convey how soon I needed it filled.

> Stop and Consider: Notice I mentioned the gas stove because self-described foodies such as myself would happily pay a small premium to have a gas stove versus electric. Some people don't care, but for others, it is a big selling point and it takes hardly any additional effort. For those people looking for something that is all-electric, this gets them moving on to the next listing right away and never wastes a second of your time.

In my second paragraph, I restated the rent amount and addressed the deposit, then detailed the expectations for the move in. I seldom require people to pay first and last month's rent plus deposit, but if people are prepared to pay that up front it lessens the sticker shock if it turns out they have a bad rental history and I decide they are an acceptable risk. Also, notice my choice of words "non-refundable pet fee" which is utilized to treat for fleas after someone with a pet moves out. My verbiage about pets is a bit vague on purpose, since you might choose to allow pets in one particular property, but not another.

Ideally, you will have your toll-free number on all your ads, from your yard signs to your listings in the newspaper or online. When someone calls that number and they select the property, if they want to speak to you, the call logic in Grasshopper can then forward their call to your cell phone during whatever hours you like. This will prevent you from getting calls during critical times at work, during dinner time, or on Sunday when you're spending time with family. If it is during those times, they will be directed to leave a voicemail which you can return the next business day.

Having this system in place immediately gave me back at least two hours each day and sometimes even more when I had numerous vacancies. At the very least, I finally had some control about when my phone would ring, and that felt incredibly liberating.

Before we close out this chapter, I'd like to leave you with one final thought. It was mentioned earlier that you will want to work towards having a website and mentioning the web address in the call script. When you have ample photos stored in your property management software, and that software is linked to your website showing your available units, you should certainly mention your website throughout your script. Many people will only call on properties where they can see interior photos. Having a website that you can direct them to not only makes you look more professional, it's much more likely to lead to serious inquiries from those who are ready to rent instead of a bunch of tire-kickers just looking around.

Infrastructure

Chapter Ten

Retire Your Cell Phone

Technology can be our best friend, and technology can also be the biggest party pooper of our lives. It interrupts our own story, interrupts our ability to have a thought or a daydream, to imagine something wonderful, because we're too busy bridging the walk from the cafeteria back to the office on the cell phone.

- Steven Spielberg

You and your friends are out having a nice time at dinner. You keep your cell phone in your pocket, as always, checking it from time to time as many of us do. "No missed calls, no texts," you say to yourself, breathing a sigh of relief. Maybe it would actually be a quiet evening? Before the thought has even left your head, your phone goes off.

Only, it's not a phone call or text message; rather, it's your voicemail notification. "How odd," you think to yourself, "My phone didn't even ring…" You excuse yourself from the table and one of your friends rolls her eyes, "Are you serious right now?"

she calls out. "Can't you have just one night where that thing isn't glued to your head?"

Smiling, you hold up your finger gesturing your friend to hold on as your heart sinks "You have fourteen new messages". Your voicemail plays:

> "Hi, this is Bob, your tenant at 101 Main Street, and we have water dripping from our ceiling. I think the tenant upstairs left the water running. I went upstairs and knocked on their door but no one answered. Please call as soon as you can."

The messages quickly go from bad to worse.

> "Hi, it's Bob again at 101 Main Street. I really need you to call me, I'm not sure why you're not picking up your phone, but this is an emergency. The water went from a drip to a steady stream from the ceiling and we don't know what to do. We have a bucket underneath it but we're afraid to go to bed in case it gets worse. Please call!"

Then from worse, they go to terrible.

> "Ok, so our kitchen is completely flooded and is now covering all the wood flooring you had installed last year. It's already starting to swell and we don't know what to do or why you aren't answering your phone..."

Hanging up, you don't even want to hear the next eleven messages; you don't even know where to start. You spent $4,500 having that new wood floor installed about a year ago. For some reason, your phone didn't ring and you aren't even showing any missed calls. Cell phones – ugh! Technology is wonderful, that is, when it works.

Unfortunately, this was very similar to a true story I experienced. The only difference was in my case, it was sewage instead of clean water. Yes, it was as bad as it sounds.

We have all had this happen to us, whether we're trying to call a friend and they don't get the message right away, or the call goes straight to voicemail when you call them. While cell phones offer us a level of convenience we didn't get to enjoy until the past decade or so, relying on them as your *only* source of contact from your customers is a recipe for disaster. From an IT perspective, this is known as a single-point-of-failure.

Cell phone towers and systems occasionally go down, which renders useless the only way for your customers to contact you. Plus, you have to consider that from time to time you need to shut your cell phone off or you're just in a bad cell reception area. What happens when you're on a plane? Or at a funeral? Or visiting a sick friend in the hospital?

The point I'm making here is that life happens outside of your real estate business. In fact, life *should* be happening outside of your business. That's the whole point of being in business for yourself, right? As I mentioned in the opening pages of this book, you likely got into this business so you could have a better life – to have the time and money to do that which excites you.

The Other Half of the Automation Story

The other half of your phone system architecture is removing the fragile cell-phone-only system you currently have in place. Don't get me wrong, cell phones are valuable tools and have certainly made our lives easier in the past twenty years. But as in the real-world example I gave you, sometimes cell phones just don't work. Not to mention, they get dropped, they break, they fall into buckets of paint, or they simply die and never come back on again. Plus, let's not forget that mobile phones are, well, mobile. This means they can be lost, stolen, or left someplace. One time I left my cell phone charging in my car overnight and didn't realize it until the next morning when I went to look for it. When I finally realized where it was, I was sick at the thought of what I was going to find when I looked. I did have a few missed calls but I was fortunate to find nothing urgent was requiring my immediate attention.

At this point, I wasn't quite ready to take the leap into an office yet, but I needed to *sound* like I had one. This was right around the time that cell phone companies could no longer hold your phone number hostage if you wanted to switch carriers. At the time, I had the same cell phone number for about ten years and changing the number would have been a nightmare. Fortunately, I could transfer my cell phone number over to a landline and get a new cell phone number that was not made public to my tenants and vendors. This move alone started saving me a tremendous amount of time and was a huge part in regaining control over my day. This eventually enabled me to hire a gatekeeper to handle the calls so I could stop trying to multitask and stay focused on higher level work.

Many people feel they must multi-task because everybody else is multitasking, but this is partly because they are all interrupting each other so much.

- Marilyn vos Savant, holder of the Guinness Record for the highest IQ score of 228

Stop and Consider: One of the things I wished I'd learned earlier in my professional career was the ability to manage interruptions. As my workload increased, I thought the answer was to learn to multitask. In my college days, I specifically remember my professors and academic advisors telling me to put multitasking as a skill on my resume. As an employer, I call this out as the bullsh*t that it is. Multitasking is a myth.

Consider this: Can you talk on your cell phone and drive at the same time? Some of us can, sure. But can you return email, talk on the phone, watch television, all while eating lunch? For those of you who say yes, I will tell you you're wrong. I know I'm trying to undo years of people telling you that multitasking is a good thing in a few short paragraphs, but follow me for a second.

The reality is that we are predators. Our eyes are firmly planted on the front of our heads so we can focus on our prey. I will concede that women tend to handle multiple tasks coming at them better than men, but ultimately, all of us are at least 300% more effective if we focus on doing one task at a time. Multiple, independent studies show this to be true. Still don't believe me? Just search online "multitasking is a myth" and read to your heart's desire. One study even tested a group of people that considered themselves "good" at multitasking. The reality was that test subjects were about as effective at accomplishing simple tasks as members of the control group who were high on marijuana. (*REFERENCE: A multitasking study performed by the Institute of Psychiatry at the University of London studying 1,100 subjects at a British firm.*)

The problem is that the start/stop/start process that happens when shifting gears from one task to another is simply rough on our brains. It can take as long as 18 minutes after an interruption for us to regain our concentration and get back to our original task. By staying focused on what you're doing – one thing at a time – not only are you three times more effective at what you're doing, but the studies also show you're also much more likely to be satisfied with the work you are getting accomplished.

VOIP Phone Systems

With the goal of sounding like a big-shot, I looked into VOIP (Voice Over Internet Protocol) phones due to their affordability and flexibility. With the technology advances in the past few years, I highly recommend considering a VOIP phone from Ring Central or FreedomVoice (www.RingCentral.com and www.FreedomVoice.com). I went with the latter of the two and I will say that their customer service and technical support is superb. Here are some things you should ask in your search for a phone service provider:

-   What kind of support do you offer? 24 Hour support is a requirement. If a company does not have this, I would move on to another provider.

-   What kind of training do you offer? This is important to learn the functionality of the system, how to set up the call logic, and many other basics as your needs expand.

-   Do I have to purchase the phones from you, or can I buy unlocked phones and have you service them? You can often buy used phones on eBay or Amazon for a third of the cost of new ones.

- Do you offer recording of inbound and outbound calls? A definite MUST, more on this later.

- How can I find the recordings I need after the fact? Very important, as most times you'll need to find calls from months or years in the past.

- Do I have the ability to see other extensions if they are in use? As of this writing, FreedomVoice does not currently have this capability, which is a pain once we had multiple extensions in an office where coworkers could no longer see one another. Not a deal-killer, but definitely annoying if you're trying to ring another extension and you can't tell if they're busy on the phone with someone else.

- Do you offer e-fax, both sending and receiving? This will prevent you from having to have a fax machine in your office, and allow you to view faxes without having to be at a physical location.

If nothing else, the take-away from the last two chapters is that aside from your website, the phone system is the first impressionable infrastructure your customers will experience. Don't go about it half-baked; be intentional with it. Through the phone-system answering script, we will communicate your business hours, where to call in cases of emergency, your website address, and set the overall tone of your business to your customers. Even if you only have one phone line, a VOIP system could allow you to have your residents press "One" for example, if they are having a maintenance emergency. This call could then be routed to your Virtual Assistant (VA).

Here is a sample phone script you can adopt for your VOIP phone:

It's a fantastic day! Thank you for calling ABC Rentals. Office hours are from 8am to 5pm, Monday through Friday, and Saturdays by appointment.

If you are looking for a place to live, please check our website at ABCRentals.com

If you are a current resident and are having a maintenance emergency, please press One.

> (Route this to your Virtual Assistant or possibly an Answering Service)

If you are looking for a place to live, please press Two.

> (Send these calls to your Grasshopper system)

If you would like to speak to someone in the office, please press Zero.

> (These calls should be sent to your Virtual Assistant)

Thanks again for calling ABC Rentals! We're building communities one Resident at a time!

The VOIP phones are fantastic for forwarding phone calls and physically moving the phone to wherever you have a broadband connection, and no one is the wiser. This usually only requires an internet connection and a little understanding of how to forward the calls. If you're not particularly tech-savvy, you can call and tell the technical support staff what you're trying to accomplish and they will take care of this for you.

The next chapter discusses the use of other people, specifically Virtual Assistants, to direct the phone calls to, in addition to handling many other tasks on your behalf. The point is to direct the phone traffic away from you, whether toward someone else or an automated message, to handle the basic questions and issues that come up. If you route any of those extensions directly to you, especially the after-hours or emergency extension, your residents will quickly figure out how to get in touch with you at all hours. This completely defeats the purpose of building this infrastructure in the first place. If you need to take calls in this manner in the beginning, that's fine, just work towards setting boundaries as soon as you can. Setting boundaries and keeping them is a pre-requisite to being among the Time-Wealthy.

Infrastructure

Chapter Eleven

Using Others to Leverage Time

**With audacity one can undertake anything, but
not do everything.**

- Napoleon Bonaparte

In my journey of developing infrastructure and processes for my business, I made quite a few mistakes. One mistake in particular cost me a ton of time and money, not to mention causing me an excess of aggravation. I knew I needed to leverage my time better. I also knew I needed to have someone else do the lower-end work that was costing me money, as opposed to doing it all myself. This much I had figured out. What I hadn't figured out was the best way to do that.

Drunk on the successes of my toll-free information line, my PM software, and implementation of QuickBooks, I made another big leap. Without a whole lot of thought, I rented a single-room office and hired my first employee. Here's where the wheels came off the wagon, so to speak.

Having an office and an employee isn't inherently a bad idea, I was just nowhere near ready for an office and had no ability to manage an employee. Truth be told, I could barely manage myself and my own time, I had no business trying to manage someone else's. Not only that, I really had no need for a physical office space at that point.

Bringing someone into my organization with no clear vision as to what she would be doing was a disaster. Simply pushing her into my new office, yelling "Do Work!" then running out of the room was not going to improve the state of things for me. She had no idea of what to do or how to help because I had given no thought to which tasks I could delegate to her. Everything I did was either in my head or done on the fly.

The processes in place were a hodgepodge of ideas created by me reacting to the biggest crisis going on at the moment. Nothing was down on paper. Having an unmanaged employee who was unclear about her role, sitting in an office I didn't really need, only added to the chaos instead of reducing it. When you factor that in with all the additional costs involved, well, it was just a mess.

Training Wheels

At the time, Virtual Assistants (VAs) weren't nearly as prolific as they are now. The good news is that not only do you have a lot of choices, but competition in the marketplace has driven the quality of service up and the prices down. Hiring a Virtual Assistant would have been a much better choice for me at that point had I known more about them.

For those of you unaware of what Virtual Assistants are capable of, imagine everything you need in an assistant that doesn't require someone's physical presence. If you really think about it, there are very few situations in back office operations that would necessitate this. In the beginning stages, it may require a little creativity to work with a VA, but as you scale up your operation, the use of Virtual Assistants can be a great way to delegate lower-end or repetitive tasks which can free up you and your employees to do higher-end work, usually at a much lower cost.

> Stop and Consider: When considering costs, keep in mind that having employees requires you to carry Workman's Compensation insurance as well as pay Employment Taxes. Not to mention the cost of benefits you'd provide as an employer. Your CPA can help you determine the true cost of an employee, although you may need to contact an insurance provider for an estimate of work comp costs in your area. For a VA, their individual rate is all you pay. Check with your CPA to see if they need to fill out a W-9 for you to avoid any potential tax liability. A blank W-9 can be downloaded for free at www.irs.gov.

Some examples of what Virtual Assistants can do:

- Answering and initiating phone calls
- Drafting and returning emails
- Creating spreadsheets
- Product research
- Competitor research
- Market research
- Setting and scheduling appointments
- Answering client questions from an online FAQ
- Taking messages
- Routing urgent phone calls
- Paying bills and other bookkeeping
- Drafting letters and legal notices
- Updating websites
- Social media management

The first thing you need to know is that all VAs and VA firms are not created equal. Some VAs do bookkeeping and some don't. Some answer phones and book appointments and others do not. Everyone's specific needs are different, so to suggest one over another would be pointless. Do your own research. Look for a VA to fill in your weak areas and can do tasks which aren't the highest and best use of your time. Or quite plainly, the work you don't like to do.

> Stop and Consider: Later on, we will talk about getting your VA set up to make phone calls for you. Ask your VA if they record outbound calls done on your behalf. This is important so you can monitor client interactions and make sure your VA isn't saying things or making promises that are contrary to what you want.

Here are some places to start, but don't hesitate to do your own research and shop around further:

Non Real-Estate Specific VAs

- International Virtual Assistants Association – http://ivaa.org/ This website has a directory of Virtual Assistants you can search by basic functions you're trying to cover. For example, some of the relevant things you can search for cover VAs who offer Accounting and Bookkeeping, Live Phone Answering, Mailing Services, Marketing and Advertising, and Real Estate Support. There's also a host of other things your VA can take care of for you. Start with this website and interview several VAs to see how they might be able to support you.

- CC: My Admin Virtual Assistants – www.ccmyadmin.com This US-based company is relatively new to the VA scene, but it seems to be a fantastic site for the low-volume user. They will only charge for the time spent on the phone or doing work for you, as opposed to purchasing blocks of time that you use in the future. Their services are vast and include all the things listed on the previous page, and certainly other things might be available upon request. They will also spend a fair amount of time matching you to the right VA for your specific needs and they take the time for onboarding as well. I highly recommend giving them a look.

- Freelancer – www.Freelancer.com   This is a great site for projects you are looking to complete and don't want to spend time on. This site also has a directory you can browse to get an idea of the services each VA offers. The nice thing about this site is that VAs are rated and reviewed based on past client experiences, so you can have a measure of comfort with what to expect when you hire them. You can also post projects to be bid upon by VAs looking for work, at no cost to you. This would be great for updating your toll-free listings, watermarking photos, posting online ads, or even creating a website for you. Their services seem to be highly focused on projects, so day-to-day operational tasks may not be a good fit for these VAs.

- Fiverr – www.Fiverr.com   This is another site you can find VAs to do all sorts of projects, too numerous to list. From building websites to creating promotional videos and doing press releases, there's someone that can work on nearly any project you may think of (and many you probably haven't thought of). I recommend browsing their site to get some ideas of what you might be able to use. Quality can vary widely, so be sure you're very clear about what it is you want, and how much you're willing to pay. Overall, I've been very happy with their service.

Real Estate Focused VAs

- Hire Smart VAs – www.HireSmartVAs.com They are a full-service VA firm specializing in the property management industry. I'm impressed with all the things they do. They not only find the VA who is a good fit for your business, they also provide training for you and for the VA as well. However, they aren't for the low-volume consumer. Costs for VAs start close to minimum wage in the United States for a full-time, fully trained person who is dedicated to your operation.

- Planet Synergy – www.PlanetSynergy.com They can do a lot of offline things, including bookkeeping. What's impressive is that they are trained in multiple Property Management software systems. The downside is that they don't answer phones or do work during normal hours in the U.S. This doesn't diminish their ability to provide adequate support though. Consider the value of having someone do work for you while you're sleeping, and waking up to find all your work orders have been charged, bookkeeping has been done, and emails have been drafted and ready for your review before they are sent.

- Real Estate Virtual Assistant Services – https://revas.us/ This seems to be a very well-run and well-organized group. They offer a variety of services for property managers. After contacting their CEO, Marshall Hatfield, he suggested I read an article they wrote about what to look for when hiring a VA for your business. A copy of the article can be found on their website. A link to that article and other useful resources is available at www.LandlordCoach.com/twiBook.

How to Hire a VA

The trick to hiring a VA is to make sure you're clear about the tasks you will want them to perform. As you evolve and learn to utilize your VA, that task list will grow, but start with the basics. Interview several VAs and make sure they can perform the tasks on your list and ask them what other things they can do. This conversation will be helpful when determining what other tasks you can delegate to them. Remember, you don't know what you don't know at this point, so let them teach you.

At a minimum, I'd suggest that they are able to answer the phone and handle basic email and document preparation, which shouldn't be a problem to find. Once you hire a VA, start them out on smaller tasks that are of little consequence if not done correctly. Consider tasks such as drafting responses to emails that come in, for example. This will require you to share login credentials to grant access to the online email portal, so be sure to use a password that you won't mind giving to your VA. After the VA drafts an email, it should remain in the "Draft" folder until you review them. If the responses are acceptable, then you can hit "Send". If not, you have an opportunity to train your new VA. Either way, you can use this experience to have your new VA develop a good FAQ (Frequently Asked Questions) to reference in the future. The FAQ will be slow to develop in the beginning, but the time investment now will be worth it in the end when you don't have to manage every little issue that comes up. Obviously not all situations will fit neatly into a FAQ, but you'll be surprised how many will once you have a sound process in place and your expectations are absolutely clear.

These interactions with your VA will help instruct them on how you think and train you in how to direct people to work for you. Managing others isn't a natural skill for most entrepreneurs, and many have little to no experience in dealing with subordinates.

This is a great way to learn to delegate with training wheels before utilizing services of others full-time.

Tasks to Delegate to your Virtual Assistant

I know for some of you the thought of turning over things to a person you've never met, or even seen for that matter, can be terrifying. This is why I suggest you start small. When thinking of the tasks to send to your VA, consider some of the reasons people contact you now. I'm betting that, in most cases, callers really don't care if they speak to you as long as they speak to someone who can handle their issue. Since we've already automated the prospecting function with our toll-free information line, it's quite likely the next annoying time-suck comes with handling maintenance requests. As I mentioned in the previous chapter, I suggest you start routing these calls to your VA instead of your cell phone.

My next few examples are more about process than infrastructure, but understanding what a VA can do for you is important. Consider the real benefit to routing calls to your VA first, rather than to you as the default. The VA can determine for you if the call is a true emergency based on a pre-made list of "emergencies" you've created in advance. In a few hours, you could create a simple "if-then" flowchart to handle nearly any emergency. "If" the resident has no heat or air conditioning, "then" the VA calls your chosen, pre-approved HVAC contractor and dispatches them. "If" the person has a water leak, "then" the VA calls the pre-approved plumber and dispatches them. "If" the person gets locked out of their home, "then" the VA calls a locksmith to get them in their home after providing sufficient identification, which is then charged to the resident according to the terms of their lease.

So you say, "Well, this is all fine and dandy during the day, but what about after-hours maintenance calls?" Of course, not all VAs will provide 24-hour phone answering, so you may need to look at some other options for after-hours emergencies. If your VA can't handle after-hours calls, one such company that will is Apartment Lines. Check them out at www.apartmentlines.com. I find their pricing to be very reasonable for the service they offer. Their live operators will direct calls to you based on a pre-set list of criteria that you determine, in advance, to be emergencies. This will prevent callers from getting through to you at 2am when they are drunk and upset about an eviction notice they just received, for example. This service can be used more than just after-hours though. Give them a call and see if you can use them to handle issues during the day too.

Delegate, Don't Abdicate

It's nice to get a reprieve from the barrage of phone calls and pass them along to someone else. However, the fastest way to get a good VA to quit on you is to make them feel as if you've abandoned them. Yes, it's okay to delegate tasks. In fact, it's necessary to do so to achieve the Time-Wealth we are seeking. But there is a big difference between delegating and abdicating. **Do not abandon your VA!** Making them feel as if you've set them up to fail by not supporting them, or using your VA to hide from upset residents is the fast-track to losing them and going right back to handling all the phone calls yourself. Set the expectations up front regarding acceptable interruptions. For all other things, your VA should be compiling a Summary Email to send to you at the end of each day for things needing your direction or items you need to handle yourself.

In the spirit of *The E-Myth Revisited*, developing your FAQ is all about "working ON your business" as opposed to "working IN your business". For example, if your VA has an issue that needs your direction, use that opportunity to develop your FAQ and document your process. Taking 30 minutes to work with your VA – as opposed to giving the quick 2-minute answer just to get them off the phone – could save weeks of time when added up over the course of a year.

If your VA is contacting you on something that really isn't urgent, tell him it's not urgent. He may not know what you consider to be an emergency and what you don't. Resist the urge to just answer the question to get him off the phone. Explain that it's not an emergency, and to put that item in the Summary Email to be discussed at the end of the day. Have your VA keep track of such questions, and in a few weeks, you will have a good FAQ and SOP (Standard Operating Procedure) developed. These can be later used both for reference and to train future VAs as you expand, or should you ever replace the one you have.

"Don't Lose Track of What You're Doing and Why You're Doing It"

Remember your Vision. The point of routing these calls is to leave you free to do the things that are a better use of your time. This is also about establishing boundaries so your business is not running you. If your residents know that all they have to do is "press one" to get in touch with you directly, you have effectively gone right back to square one where everyone had your cell phone number. Do not go backwards! Don't, under any circumstances, give out your cell phone to anyone who is not a friend or family member. Once your new cell number is out, it will get passed around like a baby at a bridal shower. You owe it to your friends, family, and your own sanity to keep your cell phone number private.

If you do have to call a resident when you're not at the office, either block your number by pressing *67 before dialing their number, or use a virtual number. My preference would be for the latter. One easy and free service to keep your phone number secure is Sideline www.sideline.com. This allows you to send and receive calls from a virtual number which can be turned on and off. There are advanced options, for a very reasonable fee, which will allow for call logic to be turned on and off much like the functions of a VOIP phone. Call logic will allow you to send callers to voicemail or to your VA outside of certain hours, easily and automatically.

Infrastructure

Chapter Twelve

Websites and Email

**Domain names and websites are
Internet real estate.
– Marc Ostrofsky, New York
Times Best Selling Author, and
venture capitalist**

If you haven't guessed by now, if you don't have a website, I'm telling you that you need one. You may be thinking, why on earth do I need one if I only have a few rental units? Remember, you have a business, and every credible business, large or small, relies on attracting customers to their product or service. In the modern age, this is done with a website.

Not only can you use a website for telling your customers about your business, but it's also a place to detail your application process, FAQs, policies, and procedures. Also, nearly all PM software systems integrate with most website platforms. This enables you to advertise your vacant units in real-time, accept online payments, and communicate maintenance requests directly with your VA. A well-designed website can take your real estate business to a whole new level. Most importantly, it removes you as the information gatekeeper.

The cost of getting a website up and running is ridiculously cheap compared to just a few years ago. So cheap in fact, there is hardly any compelling reason for any business **not** to have a website. There are literally too many different website developers to list. I will list a few examples, but feel free to do your own shopping. Just make sure the developer will enable you to embed the source code from your Property Management software to allow for the Resident Portal, Prospect Application, and Available Vacancy window to operate. Keep in mind, you might be able to employ a VA to build a website for you as well.

GoDaddy – www.GoDaddy.com This site gives you the ability to purchase a web domain name and build a website all in one place. Prices start at $9.99 per month for a professional-looking, hosted website that will serve you well.

Wix – www.wix.com If you already have a web domain name and just need a website, this option may be for you. It's very easy to get up and running in a few minutes and is very affordable.

One final thought on the website. There are numerous things to consider when choosing a domain name, which is well beyond the scope of this book. Our goal is to set up a foundation to make your life easier and become Time-Wealthy so you can enjoy the things most important to you. If you're planning on developing your rental business into a full-scale real estate investment operation, or would like more information on selecting a domain name, please see the resources on the website www.LandlordCoach.com/twiBook.

Email

This is one area that can become a giant black hole for your time if you're not careful. For all the same reasons you don't want residents to have your personal cell phone number, you should set up an email address specific to your rental business. Do not use your personal email (or work email if you still have a full-time job) to communicate with residents.

Create an email account that uses your webpage as an extension. For example, if your business address is ABCRentals.com, then your email address should be something simple such as contact@ABCRentals.com. Your website host or a VA can set this up for you if you're not sure how. You will use this is the address for all email communications regarding maintenance requests, responses to advertising of vacant units, lease renewals, and other resident-related issues. You will be sharing the login credentials with your Virtual Assistant, so if you have a habit of re-using passwords among all your online accounts, make this one different to keep your other online accounts secure. If you don't have your website just yet, you can create an email address through Gmail or Hotmail for now.

I made the critical mistake early on of using my personal email for all my email communications with residents. Just be aware that once the genie is out of the bottle it's difficult to reverse it. Keep it private from the beginning, and you won't have to worry about issues of mixing your personal and rental-business emails.

If you have already made the mistake of combining your personal emails with that of your rental business, don't despair. You can still get your life back, though it will take a little bit of work and some discipline on your part.

First, create the email for your rental business, or if you're not sure how, have a tech savvy VA do it for you. Next, share the new email login credentials with your VA, with the expectation that she will be responsible for answering all incoming emails. Under no circumstances is your VA to copy you on an email where your personal email address is visible to the resident. Instead, you should be blind-copied (BCC) or have the email forwarded to you. You don't want the resident to think information needs to flow through you in any way; otherwise the residents will just bypass the new address and continue to email you directly. This is the behavior we're trying to correct.

Finally, set up an autoresponder on your current email that will direct your clients to your new email address. It should read something like this:

> *Thank you for your email! While I endeavor to return your emails right away, I am currently checking my emails about once a week due to operational and work commitments in the coming weeks and months.*
>
> *If you are a resident, I have since implemented a new system for my rental clients to serve you better. I ask you to send your email to* contact@ABCRentals.com *with your request. If this is an emergency, please call 555-555-5555 to speak to my assistant. This new system will allow me to work more efficiently in order to serve you better.*
>
> *Have a Great Day!*
>
> *Best Regards,*
>
> *Your Name*

For those *4 Hour Workweek* fanatics, the flavor of this email may sound familiar. It took about three months or so to get people to stop emailing me directly with issues that should have gone to my office. The phone number listed in the autoresponder message should be set up through your VOIP phone system, which was discussed in the Phone System and Virtual Assistant sections.

If residents are emailing you at your job, your employer will likely not appreciate you setting up this kind of autoresponder. If that is the case, forward the email to your VA for her to respond on your behalf. The response from your VA should include instructions that residents should now use the new address for the fastest response. Under no circumstances are you to respond to residents from your employer's email address, otherwise you'll never get them to stop. Forward the emails to your VA, and let her handle them.

By sharing your email login credentials with your Virtual Assistant, she will be able to handle the issues directly. At first, the VA will probably be contacting you about nearly everything, but this is where you need to give them some direction up front, as discussed in the Virtual Assistant chapter. In addition to giving your VA access to the business email address, they can be given access to your calendar as well. This is particularly important if you are the one doing the showings and/or the maintenance on the properties.

> Stop and Consider: Are you thinking of the ways this **could** work, or are you thinking of why this **won't** work? Be honest. The paradigm of the former makes things happen. The thought process of the latter creates excuses. You can either find a way to make it happen, or you can find a way to make an excuse. It's up to you. Members of the Time-Wealthy find ways to make things happen.

Infrastructure

Chapter Thirteen

Office Space

In Prison, you spend the majority of your time in an 8x10 cell.

At Work, you spend the majority of your time in a 6x8 cubicle.

- Unknown

"Do I really need an office?" you ask. I'd consider the infrastructure improvements we've discussed up to this point to be the bare essentials. Without them, you will become busier and busier until you get to the point where you become the bottleneck for any progress in your rental business. This is exactly what you don't want to happen.

Consider the Jacksons, who invested 25 years of toil and aggravation only to arrive at the Promised Land exhausted and beaten, with no life left in them. Every property owner longs for the mortgage stamped PAID-IN-FULL. The Jacksons ran a hard race and gave it all they had, but died at the doorstep of prosperity by turning around and selling their properties. They gave up a healthy revenue stream and triggered a huge taxable event with no plan of what to do with the lump-sum of money.

What was it all for? A pile of cash doesn't translate to Time-Wealth; it takes cash *flow* for that. The last time I checked, even jumbo CD's at most banks were paying barely 1% interest. For this couple to sell their properties simply because they couldn't mentally separate themselves from the daily burden of their rentals was an absolute shame. Even if all this couple did was to have an office outside of their home, it's likely they would have drastically reduced their stress level. At least there would be a separation between their work and home life. When all you have is a home office, you are always "on duty."

So, should you consider a dedicated office outside of your home? It depends on what your goals are ultimately, but I would vote yes for several reasons.

First, I would much rather have a place where people can come to sign their lease in a comfortable atmosphere rather than doing it at a coffee shop or at the rental property. Consider what would happen if you made a mistake when printing the lease and you needed to make a correction. For me, having residents come to my house to reprint a lease is simply not an option I would entertain. Plus, your residents are going to need a copy of their signed lease, which is easier if you have a small copier at your office versus going somewhere else. With a little searching, I'm sure you can find a one room office that would cost, at most, a few hundred dollars a month. Co-working studios have popped up all over and might be also a good option, and they nearly always have a community printer/copier you can use for a few dollars when you need it.

Second, having an office gives you credibility in an industry that is not exactly known for being credible. People throw the phrase "slumlord" around trying to be either funny or offensive.

Conducting business in an office brings you to a level of credibility many others won't have. It's also important to have a clean, professional space for when you need to have closed-door discussions with residents or to conduct other business meetings. In such situations, you want to control your space and environment as much as possible. This is nearly impossible at a coffee shop. It has the same result as meeting with your residents at the rental property, their home, as you have no idea of the potential chaos waiting for you. Barking dogs, crying babies, and children running in and out of the room will dilute your impact with the residents about violating their lease, say, because they are parking their motorcycle in their living room. Yes, that really happened.

However, a meeting called in your office automatically has a professional and serious atmosphere. There's a subconscious "getting called to the principal's office" feel to scheduling such a meeting with your residents at your office. This puts you in control of the meeting right off the bat. Furthermore, this is on your turf, not theirs. Even though the house or apartment may belong to you, it's still *their* home. In your office, it's all yours. These small details make a big difference in negotiations and will help ensure you're negotiating from a position of strength. (We'll discuss more about negotiating from strength in Part Four concerning behavior.)

Mailbox / Dropbox

An office allows for residents to drop off their rent payments in a drop box or secure mailbox located there. I'm going to say something that some of you may find absolutely shocking. Since having an office with a drop box, I have **NEVER** showed up at a resident's house to pick up rent, and I **NEVER** will. This means NEVER, EVER. They signed the lease and they know the location of my office. The minute you start down the road of in-person rent collections, it becomes an expectation and is very difficult to go back.

> Stop and Consider: For those of you that are already out driving around collecting rent, hear me out. I used to drive around and pick up rent from my residents, as if they were blessing me with their phone call, and I was to be incredibly thankful that they were graciously allowing me to pick up their rent check. Let me ask, when is the last time your credit card company came by your house and picked up the payment you owed them? Never? Well, how about your mortgage company? The electric utility? The gas company? I think you get my point.

> By doing this, my tenants had trained me, and they trained me quite well. In fact, I was as well trained as a sea lion that does tricks for fish in Orlando. I can hear the arguments now, "But if I don't go there, I'll never get my rent!" My answer: Get new tenants or retrain your current ones. It is really as simple as that. You have more productive things to do with your time, and personally driving around collecting rent checks is costing you far more than you're making.

The Well-Trained Landlord

I remember watching a real estate investment video on YouTube one night for lack of anything better to do. This particular guy owned about 30 rental units, was in his mid-fifties, and looked jaded, bitter, and angry. He had an aura that life had beaten him half to death and he was looking to exact his revenge wherever he could.

He seemed to have it all figured out when it came to the rental business. His large, untrimmed mustache was a perfect complement to the disorganized shelves and brown paneling walls behind him. His advice to his hundred or so YouTube subscribers was to never buy more rental properties than you can drive to and collect rent from in a given day. He went on to explain that tenants can't be relied upon to mail the rent payments, so make sure you're there on the first day of the month to collect the rent. I sat and scratched my head in disbelief. I guess vacations, emergencies, car repairs, or the flu somehow didn't happen on the first of the month for this guy.

The sad part was that moustache man had been trained so well by his tenants and their bad behavior that he couldn't even see it. He was Time-Weary. I felt bad for the guy, but then again, I didn't. It was his fault. His lack of infrastructure caused all this. He could have corrected it with a little effort, but I sincerely doubt he did. I'm sure he is still dutifully driving his 30-plus mile route the first of every month. What's even more sad is that his growth is constrained by his own ability to collect rent. With just a little tweaking, he could actually enjoy life instead of just living it for his rental units and being at the beck-and-call of his residents. Poor moustache man is held hostage, and he doesn't even know it. Here lives the Time-Weary Landlord.

For those of you collecting rent this way, I want you to stop for a moment and consider how much time you spend showing up, knocking on doors, and chasing down rent. Can you think of a better use for that time? I'm hoping so. If not, I suggest you rethink your vision for the future. Beyond the time component, consider how unsafe this activity is when everyone in the neighborhood knows your rent collection schedule. They are going to recognize the likelihood that you'll be carrying a good amount of cash on you. There are too many stories of landlords in the news getting mugged while out collecting rent. It's not only a poor use of your time, it's also dangerous.

Bottom line: Don't let your tenants steal time from you, and don't risk criminals stealing money from you. Start training your residents. If you're currently collecting rent in person now, send each of them a letter informing them of this addition to your business infrastructure, outlining your new drop box policy. For those I knew would be resistant to the idea, I hand-delivered the letter to them. After installing a drop box at my office, I sent one to each of my residents with the following message:

Dear [Resident],   DATE

I want to thank you for being a valued customer. I apologize for having to make an adjustment to a policy which was started as a courtesy but has now evolved into an expectation. Due to the recent rise in fuel costs and changes in my schedule and work demands, I won't be able to come by and pick up the rent any longer. Starting next month, rent needs to be in my mailbox no later than the 3rd day of the month or it will be subject to a late fee in accordance with the lease.

For those of you preferring to drop off your rent, I now have a drop box for your convenience. The drop box is located at the address listed at the bottom of this letter. Please do not deposit cash as I won't be able to guarantee proper credit to your account.

I realize this will be as much as an adjustment for you as it will be for me. However, it is necessary to focus my time on more pressing matters, and to serve you better. Thank you for your understanding. Have a wonderful day!

Best Regards,

Mark Dolfini
215 S. 18th Street
Lafayette, IN 47905

I held my breath as I dropped the stack of 90 or so letters in the mail, already envisioning the mass of angry phone calls to come pouring in. In reality? Nothing happened.

Several people called me on the first of the month wanting directions to my new office and 90% of them paid their rent on time. The 10% who didn't pay on time rarely paid on time anyway. I found with the time I saved, I could make phone calls, asking the late-payers when I could expect the rent to be paid. I was also able to generate and mail late notices, which took me all of an hour.

The whole process of driving around used to take me *two full days* – a full sixteen hours or more. Plus, there was no guarantee I would catch them at home or if they would even come to the door when I knocked. It was such a monumental waste of time. Now I could remove my emotion from the entire process and focus my energy on other things. I was immediately ten times happier, and much more effectively using my time.

Infrastructure

Chapter Fourteen

Managing Risk

Lawsuits are the newest form of lottery.

- Advertisement for Legal Services

As you continue to gain momentum as a Time-Wealthy Investor, other people will start to take notice. Unfortunately, some people who notice will not have your best interests in mind and some might even seek to destroy all you've built. There are several ways to protect yourself from the inevitable lawsuit that will come your way. In business, it's often not a question of *if* you will be sued, but *when.* Most times, such lawsuits are small and are simply a nuisance you must deal with. However, you should prepare yourself adequately for risks that can ruin you financially, and keep you from realizing your vision of being among the Time-Wealthy. As a good friend of mine in the insurance industry once told me, don't worry too much about the $1,000 loss – worry about the $1,000,000 loss.

Insurance

Up to this point, the only type of insurance that you might have is your property coverage. There are several additional types of insurance you at least need to consider, some of which I would consider mandatory.

Landlord Policy

This should be obvious. A landlord policy is sometimes referred to as a "fire policy," which is different from a homeowner's insurance policy. A typical landlord policy covers the loss of the property and sometimes the loss of rent revenue. One key difference is that homeowners' policies cover contents, whereas a landlord policy only covers contents owned by you and your company, not the tenant's contents. If you are converting the use of a house you once lived into a rental, be sure not to overlook getting the proper coverage in place.

There are two standards insurers use when reimbursing policyholders for their losses: Actual Cash Value and Replacement Cost.

> Actual Cash Value (ACV) – A policy using this standard is generally going to have lower premiums, and is sufficient if you can self-insure to a certain extent. Self-insuring is having access to money, such as savings or credit, to help offset some of the risk. A policy using ACV as the standard pays the depreciated value of whatever has been damaged. Let's say a windstorm causes part of your roof to take a dip in the neighbor's pool. With ACV, the age of the roof will be considered when paying the claim. Keep in mind that this standard may be your only option on older properties.

Replacement Cost (RC) – Insurance with this repayment standard is usually going to be more expensive because it's typically considered better coverage. The reason for the higher premium reflects the fact that the insurer will pay the claim, without factoring in depreciation. In the case of the roof that blew away, the age of the roof would not matter. The insurance company will pay to have it restored to the original condition; all you would pay is the deductible.

Personal Umbrella Policy

A good friend of mine, Jan, is an Allstate representative. Jan has a knack for assessing risk, and she turned me onto this type of insurance. A personal umbrella policy helps cover things that might be missed by other types insurance. Overall, this helps cover personal liability that a General Liability policy may not specifically cover. For personal asset protection, this is a great idea, and the cost is quite reasonable.

Renter's Insurance

The renter purchases this insurance to protect their personal belongings, as well as some liability coverage. It's important that your residents have this sort of coverage for several reasons, not the least of which is to hold a resident accountable if they cause damage to your property, such as a fire or flood. Plus, your landlord policy does not cover their contents (furniture, electronics, clothing, etc.), so encourage them to purchase this type of insurance, which is relatively inexpensive.

Stop and Consider: It is important for your renters to have this coverage to help manage your own risk. Take for example, the tenant causes a fire at your property. The benefit to you is in the event of a claim, your insurance company will pursue the renter's policy on your behalf. This process between the insurance companies is known as subrogation. Don't just think of fires though, think of all things that the resident owns that could cause damage to persons or property: biting dogs, leaking fish tanks and window air conditioning units, for example. Consider the things that they do as well such as clogging toilets and getting the heat shut off in the winter causing the pipes to freeze.

Policy Exclusions

I can't stress this enough: Pay attention to what the policy does NOT cover. Policy exclusions are the insurance company's way of minimizing responsibility for paying claims. Don't think of exclusions as necessarily being a bad thing. Policy exclusions allow the insurer to provide you the coverage you want and nothing more, thereby making your coverage more affordable. Carefully review the exclusions and make certain you understand what type of losses you're covered for and what type you're not.

Here are some examples of exclusions you can expect to see on any given policy:

- Intentional Loss
- Flood Insurance
- Water and Sewer Backup
- Mold
- Governmental Authority
- Earthquake
- Terrorism
- War
- Nuclear Hazard
- Riots, Civil Disturbance
- Pest / Animal Control

- Theft by Employees
- Vandalism
- Normal Wear and Tear
- Corrosion
- Mechanical Breakdowns
- Environmental Pollution
- Faulty Workmanship
- Vacancy

Insurance carriers differ immensely. While there are some fundamental similarities, there are also many differences in how they underwrite policies and approach risk. That's why it's important to shop around. Of course, you should look at the rate, but consider the likelihood they will pay a claim, should one come up, and what you can expect if you need to interact with them.

Two sites you can look at to see how your insurer stacks up against the rest:

J.D. Power – www.JDPower.com Here you can search insurance companies and see how they compare on six different areas of consumer interest: Policy Offerings, Price, Billing, Interaction, Claims, and Overall Satisfaction.

Better Business Bureau – www.BBB.org The ratings for companies will vary from A+ to F, and are based on a set of standards used across all industries. This is a handy website for gauging how customers are treated. By reading reviews and complaints, you can see problems other customers have run into. Understand that all companies make mistakes. Unfortunately, there is a complaint-side-bias on sites like this since very few people go out of their way to post a positive review if they've been treated fairly or are satisfied customers.

Make sure you have the appropriate coverage to protect your assets. It's equally important to understand that almost anything can be insured. It just depends on what you're willing to pay, and if the insurer is willing to underwrite it. If you want insurance for any of the exclusions listed above, you can purchase a rider for that specific exclusion. If your insurer doesn't offer coverage for that exclusion, you can usually get coverage from a different insurer.

Insurance Agents

Just as all insurance carriers are not alike, neither are insurance agents. There are captive agents who work for just one insurance company, and independent agents who represent several different insurance carriers. A captive agent may represent only Allstate or State Farm, for example. These companies only allow their agents to sell their products. An independent agent, by contrast, usually has more flexibility because they can choose from different carriers they represent, such as Erie, Progressive, and Foremost, to name a few.

Don't simply go by what your agent tells you; instead, **read the policy and understand what is in it**. There are a lot of great agents out there, but you need to watch out for your own interests, not the interest of the insurance salesperson. I'm not suggesting that your agent is a liar or a moron, but they do make mistakes, and some of those mistakes could cost you a lot of money. At the end of the day, your agent represents a carrier, and it won't matter what he or she "told you" when you have a claim. What **will** matter is what is written in the policy. So, I can't stress this enough, **read the policy and understand what is in it!** If you don't understand what you're reading, get a trusted third party such as another insurance agent or attorney who speaks the insurance language and can help you interpret what it all means.

Long story short: Make sure you have the coverage you need and you understand the exclusions. If you don't have the coverage you want, get it in place before you need it.

Proof of Insurance from your Vendors

When hiring subcontractors, do not allow them to perform any work for you until they provide you with a copy of their General Liability policy. Most small businesses have policy coverages from $1 million to $3 million. To manage your own risk, check with your own insurance agent to see what coverage level he or she recommends your subcontractors have. If you're not going to be doing work for others, it's not likely that you would need a General Liability policy for yourself. Just check with your insurer or attorney to make sure you are adequately protected.

> Stop and Consider: Worker's Compensation Insurance is easy to overlook if you've never had employees. It is important coverage in case someone on your payroll gets hurt while they're on the job; and it's required by law. **Don't put this off!** If you know you're going to hire someone, start contacting insurers right away and ask them if they provide Work Comp and General Liability insurance. If you aren't sure if you need this coverage, check with your insurance agent or attorney.

Legitimate subcontractors should be able to provide you a copy of their Work Comp insurance without question or difficulty. If they are a sole proprietor, as are many mom-and-pop operations providing handyman services, they may be able to opt-out of the state's Work Comp requirement. Every state is somewhat different, and some states may not allow this at all. This can be researched and the opt-out can often be performed online through your State's Secretary website.

This is important to you is because if a subcontractor does not have this coverage in place, and one of their employees gets hurt while on a job for you, they can potentially come back on you for their injuries and lost wages. I know this sounds like a raw deal, but it can happen. Just make sure they have the proper coverage before they do any work.

To Incorporate or Not to Incorporate

Setting up a corporate entity for your rental business may make sense, but be sure you understand why you're doing it. Most landlords choose to either set up a corporate entity either as an LLC (Limited Liability Company) or as an S-Corporation, but those aren't the only choices under which you can operate. Your other choices could be as a Sole Proprietor, an LLP (Limited Liability Partnership), and a C-Corporation.

Limited Liability Companies (LLCs) and S-Corps offer certain liability protections as well as tax advantages. However, they are not the same. It is important to know the difference and what would be the best structure for you, your strategy, where you're going, how you would be protected, and what impact it could have on your taxes.

I interviewed Tressa Heath, a CPA and author, for this book. We got into a lengthy discussion about setting up a corporate entity for rental properties. She offered one piece of advice which overrides all others: Talk to a CPA first. Everyone's tax situation is different, and while I do suggest talking to an attorney as well, a CPA will more completely understand how establishing a legal entity will impact you from a financial perspective.

Most landlords usually start as a sole proprietor and consider setting up a corporate structure after the fact. There are some benefits to being a sole proprietor, one being very low administrative costs, but there are significant drawbacks as well. The most obvious downside to operating as a sole proprietor is the potential for liability on your personal assets. This means, if you are sued, you are risking not only the assets of your business, (your rental property, tools, vehicles, and equipment) but also your personal assets such as your home, car, and bank accounts. This is why it's so important to have the proper insurance coverage in place. Having a corporate structure for your rental business could shield your personal assets as well.

> **I busted a mirror and got seven years bad luck, but my lawyer thinks he can get me five.**
>
> **- Steven Wright, Comedian**

Hiring an Attorney

Most attorneys who work on landlord-tenant cases are easy to find; just visit an eviction court the next time it's held in your area, which for most areas is daily. I suggest calling around and talking to a few different attorneys to see who is accepting new clients and who you would like to work with. You can also talk to some other landlords and property managers in the area to see who they use.

Here are some basic questions to ask when considering hiring an attorney:

- Do you focus your practice on landlord-tenant cases?

  Many attorneys will limit their law practice to a few key areas. I'd be a little wary of attorneys who do many areas of law since there is so much to know from one to the next. Landlord-tenant laws vary in many areas and, like many laws, are constantly evolving. I'd prefer to hire an attorney who keeps up with these changes and works in this field often over one who does it only occasionally.

- Do you do collections? If so what do you charge?

  It is far more convenient to have the same attorney who does your evictions and legal work to do your collections. Many will work on contingency, which means they don't get paid unless you get paid. I've seen rates vary from thirty percent to one-half of the collected amounts. If there are out of pocket costs, such as court-filing fees, those are generally paid up front.

- What are your rates and how do you charge?

  Many attorneys in this industry will charge anywhere from $200 an hour on up. It does pay to shop around, but keep in mind you do get what you pay for. Don't let the rate alone be the determining factor as many will bill you in 15-minute increments for their time. Ask them what you could expect to pay for them to represent you in court if you had to file for an eviction or had a hearing to get a judgement for damages.

- What will you need from me if we have to file an eviction?

  This will largely depend on the court in which you file for your evictions. Each court is run a little differently depending on the judge who oversees it. Keep in mind, in most areas, judges are elected and are replaced from time to time. The way a court runs under one judge does not mean it will run the same under another.

- Are you available for me to ask questions about leases and other contracts?

> Just like your CPA, use the *Good to Great* paradigm and consider your attorney one of the people on your bus. You'll need this person to answer various legal questions which arise from time to time. Any attorney familiar with contract law and leases should be able to help you with whatever comes up in your real estate business.

Getting the Most Value

The best way to get the most value from your attorney is to respect her time. Don't call her office and have a 15-minute chit-chat session about the weather before getting to the point. You don't need to be a jerk about it, but exchange pleasantries and say something like "Well, I want to be respectful of your time, so if you need to start the clock on my bill that's okay with me."

Have your questions already written out before you call and be clear about why you're calling. Even better, send an email to your attorney in advance with an overview of what you'll be discussing. This will allow her to adequately prepare if it's a topic where she needs to do some research. Attorneys get paid for their knowledge and opinions, so be respectful of their time when you interact with them, and they will be respectful of your wallet.

This is the end of the section on Infrastructure. Taking time to lay the foundation of infrastructure for your business now will save countless hours of aggravation later. Next, we begin to incorporate different processes upon the foundation you just built.

Part II – The Power of Process

Chapter Fifteen

The Basics

Real Estate cannot be lost or stolen nor can it be carried away. Purchased with common sense, paid for in full, and managed with reasonable care it is about the safest investment in the world.

- Franklin D. Roosevelt

Jack spent the last few weeks putting many things in place for his business. Several weeks ago, Jack and his wife stopped off at a few different places before going to dinner. Subway, Burger King, Taco Bell, and Office Depot in particular. Going in to look around, Jack's intent wasn't to buy anything. Instead, he looked for similarities in each of their infrastructures to replicate within the framework of his own business. He thought how amazing it was that he always had a similar experience no matter which of these stores he visited. Infrastructure is hard to see, he thought. It seemed only to be noticed when it was either broken, or not there at all.

He observed the processes running on the infrastructure within each business. He keenly scrutinized the process used by every cashier and examined how each of those processes varied, depending on the infrastructure upon which they ran. It was a lesson in business-forensics, and Jack was taking it all in.

Armed with the information gathered from his field trip, Jack spent the next month researching PM software to help him operate more efficiently and effectively. He also set about hiring a CPA who would get his finances on track, opting to forego accounting software for the moment. He felt that his final choice of CPA could help him pick one and get it set up, if Jack decided to go that route. His choice of CPA cost him $250 to review his finances and make sure he could get the financial data he needed to make good decisions. Jack learned that he needed to account for things in a certain way, and the CPA would make sure it was done properly.

His next step was setting up a phone system so he could get some much-needed relief from his cell phone. He wasn't sure exactly how it was going to work, but a friend of his had been using Virtual Assistants to answer the phone at his dry-cleaning business during peak hours, and Jack thought he could do something similar. Jack also considered how he could automate some of his inbound calls during the work day by setting up an account on Grasshopper.com. His wife, excited by seeing Jack spending time working *on* his business as opposed to *in* his business, offered to voice the messages for the available vacancies. Jack was laying the groundwork for much more free-time in his life and was gaining momentum. With some basic infrastructure in place, Jack set about creating sound processes in which to operate.

> **Efficiency is doing things right; effectiveness is doing the right things.**
>
> - Peter Drucker

The Basics of Process

With your infrastructure in place, you are ready to start putting the Process-Expectations-Behavior method into practice for your business. As you're developing processes, put in place only those things related to getting you closer to your vision. This isn't always easy to do because we often become emotionally invested in processes where there is little value to the customer. For example, does it make sense to send out birthday cards if you're not able to handle their maintenance requests in a timely manner? Obviously not. Imagine this from the resident's perspective:

"Sure, they have time to send me a birthday card but my refrigerator has been broken for three weeks!"

Obviously not a good situation; you can't put icing on cake batter. If you're not even accomplishing the basics, don't try to go above and beyond.

This "cutting of the fat" can be brutal. Having an absolutely clear vision of where you're going and what you're wanting to create is critical to keeping you on track. Maybe doing something like sending out birthday cards to build long-term goodwill is a must for you. However, as a business owner, you should always be asking yourself why you're doing what you're doing. If the answer is: "because this is the way I've always done it" then maybe it's time to look at things differently.

I bring this up now because we are about to set in motion several processes that you're going to have someone else run. Having a meaningless process in place that you're going to pay someone else to do is not only a giant waste of time, but an obvious waste of resources. If you're considering a process that doesn't move you one step closer to the goals you've laid out in your vision, reconsider doing it at all.

Setting your VA Up for Success

There are many ways to set your VA up for failure. Let's consider the foundation we're building and set them up for success instead. It's going to be a terrible experience for everyone involved, your residents, your VA - not to mention **you** - if your VA doesn't have the first clue how to respond to basic questions from callers. Imagine how you'd feel when you're asking seemingly innocuous questions of a staff person only to get the universally annoying retort: "I'll have to ask my manager."

Understand if they "must ask the manager" it's not their fault. Swallow your pride and realize this issue lies squarely on you. It's easy to fix though, with a little effort. A large part of setting your VA up for success lies in developing a well-thought out FAQ for them to reference.

As discussed in an earlier chapter, your FAQ is the first step in breaking the chains of monotony. Look at your FAQ two different ways. The first is from your VA's perspective to use as a helpful resource answering resident questions as they arise. The other is for the residents to reference directly, on your website for example.

To start out, have your VA simply answer the phone and take messages. These messages are then passed along to you in a Summary Email at the end of each day. You will use those emails to help your VA develop your FAQ. You can do this on the phone with your VA and have him transcribe the answers, or you can simply reply to each question on the email and send it back. Don't take this lightly. I developed a FAQ for a realtor who showed properties for me 10 years ago that I still use today.

You can go a step further and think of all the questions prospects ask when they contact you now, in addition to all the things they ask when you're showing them a property. Questions such as "Do you allow pets?" to "Can I do work in lieu of paying the

Security Deposit?" By taking the time now to come up with a list of questions and answers, based on all the things you have been asked in the past, you'll be saving countless hours of aggravating back-and-forth with your VA.

This is a good start for your Virtual Assistant. We will work on developing a solid FAQ in Part Three – Expectations. Next, we will develop a solid process for your VA concerning the properties themselves.

Property Descriptions

As you think about your call traffic, it will be necessary to develop solid property descriptions for your VA. This will enable him or her to describe property features in detail to someone who has never seen the property, such as a plumber, HVAC technician, or a person interested in renting. Be as detailed as you can in terms of the types of appliances, make, and model numbers. Take pictures, not only for marketing purposes, but for the VA to use to describe the property better. A floorplan of the property is also helpful, even if it's only hand-sketched.

Take pictures of water shut off valves, gas valves, and the main circuit breaker and their locations. Give the photos context from both close up and from across the room so they can easily be described in an emergency.

> Stop and Consider: At the property, if the main shut off valve for the water is not in a conspicuous place, I strongly recommend posting a permanent, obvious sign pointing to the exact location of the shut off valve. Be sure to physically operate the valve at least once per year as part of your annual inspection ensuring it will still actually shut off the water. Sometimes valves malfunction, so do this to avoid a potentially costly

problem that may otherwise go unnoticed until far too late.

The Power of Process

Chapter Sixteen

Virtual Assistants and Vendors

Alone we can do so little,
together we can do so much
- Helen Keller

In Part One on Infrastructure, we discussed how to hire a VA so we can delegate low-end tasks and free up our valuable time. If you haven't hired a VA yet, or if you have, but fear losing control by delegating, relax. I've been there. Yes, it's a little unnerving at first, but it's only scary because it's new. Drafting emails and taking messages is a great start. One of next easiest things to delegate with minimal amounts of screw-ups is assigning your VA to work with your maintenance vendors. The task of assigning vendors is simple, but if you're still nervous at this idea, set a dollar limit on work they are allowed to authorize, say, under $250. You'll know pretty quickly if things aren't working as planned.

Hiring Maintenance Vendors / Subcontractors

Determine to have at least three vendors in each main category to handle incoming work orders. While you can come up with many categories, the basic ones are as follows:

- Electrical
- Plumbing
- Roofing / Siding
- HVAC
- Appliances
- General Repairs / Handyman
- Lawn Care / Snow Removal / Landscaping
- Disaster restoration / Water extraction / Board-up services
- Wildlife/ Pest Control

Plus, those services you will need for turning vacancies:

- Painting
- Cleaning
- Carpet Cleaning

You can get into more detail, but I don't think it's necessary. For example, even if your landscaping person doesn't trim trees, he'll likely know someone in that industry. Plus, many handyman services can do work for you that would likely overlap into other areas. Before hiring anyone, there are a few things you should consider before bringing them on board:

- Maintenance Survey – This simple tool provides guidance to your VA as to which vendor to assign to specific tasks. When considering a subcontractor, have them fill out a maintenance survey asking them to rate themselves on over 50 different types of repairs. A "1" rating means they have no skill or interest, to a "10" meaning they are experts in that area and want to do that work. Anyone who rates themselves less than "7" in any particular area would not be assigned that task. A sample survey available for download is available at www.LandlordCoach.com/twiBook. This is important because you may find an electrician, for example, who might also be an excellent painter when things are slow for him.

- Workman's Compensation Insurance – Do not assume a vendor has coverage in place simply because they have a fleet of vehicles and 15 employees. If one of their employees gets hurt on your job, and their employer has let this coverage lapse, you could be on the hook for it. Every legitimate business should be forthcoming when you ask for proof of their work comp coverage. This should be updated each year, so get your VA in the habit of checking that you have the latest policy on file from your vendors before assigning work to them.

- General Liability Insurance – This policy covers potential damage to your property caused by the company's employees. Obtain a copy of this to ensure your exposure is limited if your vendor causes damage. Make sure the dates on the certificate of coverage show the policy is in force and have a mechanism to check for updated proof of insurance each year.

- W-9 – This form should be filled out so your accountant can send out 1099s at the end of the year. Without this information, you may get stuck with additional tax liability.

Be sure to get this from your CPA, or download it from www.irs.gov.

As for assigning tasks to your VA, start small. Provide a list of competent, reliable vendors you're already using for tasks you know they can do, such as appliance repair. Keep it simple, and follow a straightforward flowchart. First, identify how maintenance requests are to come in. Devise a straightforward way for residents to communicate both emergency and non-emergency maintenance requests to your VA. There are numerous ways for your residents to do this. Some examples:

Emergency Requests:

- Set up an extension on your VOIP line that sends callers to a live person 24-hours a day, whether it's your VA or an answering service (refer to the section on Infrastructure.)
- Set up an emergency email, Facebook Messenger profile, or text message number that is continuously monitored and responded to by your VA.

Non-Emergency Requests:

- Set up an extension on your VOIP line where residents can leave a message for non-emergency maintenance requests.
- Have residents email a resident helpdesk or call in work orders directly to your VA during business hours.
- Have residents input work order requests through the Resident Portal in the Property Management software.
- Create an online form on your website for your residents to fill out and submit.

Whatever you decide upon, I recommend making it simple and limiting the choices to only one or two options. The more choices residents have to submit maintenance requests, the more media sources that will need to be monitored creating more opportunities for things to fall through the cracks. Honestly, if there's no reason to add more choices, then don't. The only stipulation I'd suggest is that your VA must have the ability to monitor incoming messages so you don't have to. Resist the urge to become a tollbooth for information to pass through.

Obviously, each issue will have its own follow-through procedure, depending on the nature of the maintenance request. However, regardless of the issue, each work order must be entered into the work order portion of your PM software so its progress can be tracked. This is equally true of emergency calls, which we'll discuss next.

Emergency Maintenance – After Hours

How you handle this is going to depend on what level of service is available from your Virtual Assistant. VAs represented by larger firms can usually handle customer calls 24 hours a day. Smaller, one-man shops are less flexible. I would be extremely cautious of a one or two-man operation that says they offer 24-hour service. You're becoming an expert on infrastructure and process, so consider how they will accomplish this; question them directly. If they are going to rely on cell phones to do this, then you've gone back to a delicate cell-phone-only architecture and all its inherent flaws.

If your VA does offer 24-hour phone answering, that's great. Just make sure you understand their system and are comfortable with how they will convey information about your account across the different VAs in their company. If you don't have a measure of comfort with how they will accomplish both daytime and overnight calls, or if they don't offer 24-hour service, consider hiring multiple VAs – One VA to handle the after-hours calls, and another for the day-to-day operational needs. This is something you can quite easily set up in your call logic on your VOIP or virtual phone. For example, from 8am to 4:59pm, callers get routed to one VA, and from 5pm to 7:59am callers get routed to another. The same call logic can be applied on weekends too.

Another option is to use the company, Apartment Lines, discussed in the section on Infrastructure. (www.ApartmentLines.com) You can use them during the day or overnight, and have them direct calls based on what **you** determine to be an emergency, not the caller. Plus, they do a good job of providing a consistent level of service to your customers.

Consider Yourself a Maintenance Vendor / Subcontractor

If you have been physically doing all your own maintenance up to this point and plan to continue doing so, I need you to take a vow, right now. Seriously, wherever you are, sitting on your couch, riding on a train, driving in a car listening to this on audio, whatever. Raise your right hand and repeat after me:

"I am now a subcontractor."

Did you say it? No? Well say it. Say it a few more times. I need you to be okay with the fact that you're not going to be the one assigning the maintenance work anymore. You are just like every other vendor now when it comes to maintenance. Granted, you might still be the one **doing** all the maintenance, but for now, that's fine. If you're not particularly handy at fixing things then you've got nothing to worry about, and perhaps are relieved that we're putting a system in place to handle the maintenance function. For those of you that are doing this work, however, this is going to be the most difficult piece of this whole exercise. It's time to let go of the maintenance dispatching function and allow someone else to do it.

Treating yourself as a subcontractor also keeps you from becoming the bottleneck for growth in your business. If you intend to grow your business and add properties to your portfolio, sooner or later, you will not be able to keep up with the volume of maintenance headed your way. Even if you can keep up with the regular maintenance issues, major projects will arise from time to time, in addition to the turns needed when properties become vacant. If you're also doing the showings and property inspections, this can quickly get out of hand.

Considering yourself to be a maintenance vendor allows your VA to assign work orders to the appropriate vendor, even if that vendor is you for the time being. As you and your VA develop your network of trusted vendors, little by little, your VA (at your direction) will start assigning the lower-end work, and the work you're not particularly skilled at, to these trusted vendors.

The list of vendors should look something like this:

Your Name – General Handyman, 24 Hours – 555-555-5555

ABC Plumbing – Plumbing and HVAC, 24 Hours – 999-999-9999

XYZ Plumbing – Plumbing, 7am to 7pm M-F – 999-111-1111

Trusted HVAC – Plumbing and HVAC, 24 Hours – 112-222-2323

123 Appliance Repair – Appliances, 8-5 M-F, 8-Noon Sat – 222-222-2222

Rhonda Smith – Realtor, Showings, Mon-Sat 1pm to 7pm – 555-667-7777

Consider this example:

When a call comes in, your VA goes into the PM software and enters a work order for a resident's broken pipe. She looks at the list of vendors handling plumbing items based on the maintenance survey they completed and starts calling them, checking for their availability. If it's an emergency repair, based on your pre-defined list as to what constitutes an emergency, the job gets categorized as such, and anyone that is not available within say, four hours, is set aside until another vendor is found.

> Stop and Consider: In the case of a true emergency, such as an active water leak, your VA should have a set of instructions specific to each property to direct the residents to the location of the main shut off valves. This would be planned for in advance by clearly labeling the valve at the property, as well as having a detailed description written out in the PM software as to how to locate it for the VA to reference. If the resident is not able to shut off the water main, your VA should know to contact you immediately, or your emergency plumber on call, to minimize any damage.

> Some municipalities have people on call to shut water off at the outside meter in the case of such emergencies. Call the water billing office in advance and ask them if they can handle such problems. The last thing you want is for the water to run for three hours while waiting on a plumber to show up.

Normal incoming repair requests should be scheduled and completed within 72 hours. If that's not possible, consider finding another vendor for that repair. This may sound like a very compressed timeline, but maintenance is far and away the number one complaint among residents about landlords and property managers. Work orders must be taken seriously and addressed in a timely fashion. Yes, "consistency" is our goal and our product. However, "consistently slow" is not what we're shooting for.

Referring back to our example, a maintenance request comes in and your VA starts down the list of vendors, checking your availability. If you're available to do the repair, the work order is sent to you via email, and you schedule the repair with the resident. If you'd like to avoid having two cell phones, I recommend that you block your number by dialing *67 before dialing the resident's number. If you need them to call you back, instead of leaving them your cell phone number, set up an extension through the office number that forwards to your cell phone. This way your cell number stays private, and the call is also recorded when they call back. However, I'm not a fan of this because it allows residents a means to contact you whenever they want.

Another way to keep your number private is to direct residents to call the office and have them select an option that routes them through your VA. Instruct the resident to request to be connected to you directly. Your VA or answering service would then put the caller on hold, contact you, and ask if it's ok to patch the resident through to you. This method is preferred, as your VA can help you avoid taking a call that he or she could otherwise handle.

One additional option of keeping your number private is to set up a virtual number through a product called Sideline. (www.sideline.com) This is the free service mentioned earlier that allows you to have multiple numbers on one cell phone. The only downside is residents, once again, have a direct way of contacting you. However, for a few dollars a month, you can easily set the call logic on to auto reply to text messages and route all calls to a voicemail or your VA when you do not want phone calls. If you're waiting on a resident to call you back, simply turn the call logic off until the call comes in.

Final Thought

If you're not available to do the repair in a timely manner, your VA should go to the next available vendor on the list. This is why it's important to have at least three vendors for each job type. For example, having at least three plumbers, three HVAC contractors, and three disaster restoration contractors ensures you have enough depth of coverage to handle maintenance as it arises in those areas.

Once the maintenance has been scheduled, your VA should follow up with the resident, making sure the repair was performed. This will ensure the residents are taken care of satisfactorily and that the vendor is not paid for incomplete work. Do not be surprised when vendors fail to show up or do not complete a repair as promised. Most of them, especially the ones with cheap rates, will overpromise and underdeliver. Some will disappear off the face of the earth, never to be heard from again. I hate to say it, but it's fairly common. This is another reason I recommend going at least three-deep on every maintenance category. Also, I don't recommend selecting a vendor simply based on low rates. If your VA is having to spend a lot of time babysitting a particular vendor, move on to the next one. There simply comes a point where the costs far outweigh the benefits. The more you need to manage someone, the less valuable they are.

You want to be known as the person who vendors want to work for. There is a sure-fire way to get vendors to avoid working for you and that is to take an excessive amount of time getting them paid. An incredibly simple, but extremely effective way to get vendors to put you at the top of their list is to pay them quickly. I'm not suggesting you should stop all other activity and cut them a check on the spot, but they shouldn't have to wait 30 to 45 days to be paid either. Vendors, especially small mom and pop operations, have expenses they need to cover to do your job. Make it systemic so that you can inspect the completed work or confirm with the resident that the repair is complete, and get them a check in the mail or have your VA pay them with a credit card within a few days. Your vendors will love you for it, and will be eager to come back.

The Power of Process

Chapter Seventeen

Advertising and Prescreening

Trying to do business without advertising is like winking at a pretty girl through a pair of green goggles. You may know what you're doing, but no one else does.

**- Cyrus McCormick,
American Inventor**

Advertising is the key to filling your current and upcoming vacancies. This can involve anything from posting your available units online, to yard signs, to putting ads in the newspaper. Every real estate market is different, so what may work in one area may not be as effective in another.

For example, I'm not a huge fan of using the newspaper in my hometown.   It's nothing personal against hometown newspapers, or other print media for that matter. I just find it to be very expensive in my market in relation to the other types of media that attract the people I want to my available units. I used to place ads in the classifieds to run on the weekends, but I learned that having a good website and posting on Craigslist yielded much better results for me.

By contrast, in a town just 30 minutes south of my office, I run a small ad in that area's local newspaper on Friday, Saturday and Sunday, and place a sign in the yard. This approach yields far better results than anything I post online. For whatever reason, the internet just isn't as effective there. The ad and yard sign are all I need to get plenty of phone traffic.

There is no one "right way" when it comes to advertising. Being effective involves some trial and error, so if you're not getting the call volume you're hoping for, put yourself in the shoes of your prospects. Consider where you would search to find a place to live if you were looking for yourself, or perhaps ask the waitress at your local restaurant where she might look.

Here are some of the online advertising media you might consider:

> Facebook – I've never been a fan of placing my available units on Facebook, although I know many people do it. If it works for you, great! Don't stop! I've just never experienced it being an effective use of my time with all the back-and-forth with people only partially interested. If you are posting on Facebook or other social media outlets, be sure to drive people to your website and toll-free number so they can get more information on all your available properties.

> Hotpads, Trulia, Zillow, Craigslist – These are all free and effective ways to advertise your available rental units. This would be a good place to post your toll-free number in the listing as we discussed in the section covering phone systems. Make sure you cover the basics, which are often easy to miss in your haste to get the listing up and running. Use the following as a checklist so you don't miss anything:

- Property address
- Date available for move-in
- Rent amount
- Security deposit amount
- Pet policy (a simple "Some Pets Okay" or "No Pets" will suffice at this point in the process)
- Required utilities
- Appliances included
- A basic description of the property i.e. 3 bedroom, 2 bath with garage, etc.
- Your business contact information
- Photos of the outside AND the inside, particularly of the kitchen, bathrooms, appliances, and any special features you'd like to highlight. I recommend posting at least four photos, but no more than seven.

Stop and Consider: When taking photos, there are several things you need to keep in mind. Most cell phones take good quality photos, so don't feel you should buy a fancy camera just for this purpose. When at the property, try to get as much natural light behind you and don't use the flash if you can help it. The flash makes the photos look very "clinical" and almost sterile, whereas a photo using natural lighting appears warmer and more welcoming. Turn on the lights inside the home, which also gives the photos a nicer look. When photographing the bathrooms, close the shower curtains or doors if present, and be sure the lids to the toilets are down. Sometimes having the blinds open will make a good photo, and sometimes not. Do both and see what looks the best. There are several examples on the site at www.LandlordCoach.com/twiBook.

Here's an example of what an online advertisement might look like:

> Located at 123 Main Street, this is a cute 2 bedroom, 1 bath single family home with refrigerator, stove, and washer / dryer for $795 per month, with a $795 security deposit. Some small pets are okay, cats and dogs only, for an additional monthly fee of $25 per pet plus non-refundable pet fee of $150. The resident is responsible for gas, water, and electric utilities.
>
> Call 877-555-5555 for more information on this great starter home, or press '0' to speak to a leasing agent before this one gets away!
>
> NOTE: While we do our very best to ensure our advertising is accurate, we do reserve the right to make corrections to the terms, utilities, policies, pricing and amenities as we are made aware of such inconsistencies. We thank you for your understanding.

SCAM ALERT! Be warned, for any of the online sites, you have to be careful about people stealing your ads and reposting them as their own. The scam goes as follows: The scammer sees your online ad, they right-click and save all your photos onto their computer. They then create a fake profile and post the photos of your property as if it were their own, keeping everything basically the same except they put in their contact information. The dead giveaway of this scam is the substantially discounted rent price, say 40% to 50% lower than the going market rent. This ensures attracting a lot of would-be renters.

All they need is one ignorant soul to take the bait. The would-be renter contacts someone who they think is the owner to ask questions and set up a showing. The "owner", in this case the scammer, responds back with a poorly-worded and grammatically-barbaric email about how they are blessed financially to be able to offer such a nice home at a discounted rent amount. The scammer then instructs the prospect to wire them one month's rent and the keys will be sent to them in the mail. By the time the person realizes they've been scammed, the money is long gone and the scammers are on to their next victim.

This is happening over and over in all rental markets. Scammers have stolen my ads in the past, but now I will only place photos online that have my company phone number and logo watermarked right across the middle of the picture. This makes it just difficult enough so the scammers simply go on to someone else's ad that isn't watermarked.

Many types of photo editing websites and software will allow you to watermark your pictures. This is something you should have your VA do for you. I use a product called Snagit from www.techsmith.com to crop, edit, watermark and embed logos on the photos of my properties. It's not expensive software, and admittedly it may be more than you need. At a minimum though, make sure your phone number and website is bolded smack in the middle of the photo so it can't easily be cropped out.

Require them to Walk the Property in Advance

I strongly suggest you make it a policy to NOT process a rental application for someone who has not physically been to your property. Roughly half the time I processed an application from an out-of-state prospect who hadn't seen the property firsthand did the deal work out. Photos are good, videos are better, but nothing replaces the ability to physically be at a property. As desperate as some people might sound on the phone or via email, don't give in to it.

The last time this happened to me was during a tough time of year to rent houses. I had been holding this particular place vacant for nearly a month for only a few hundred dollars in earnest money. The house was cleaned, painted and ready to go. The couple was moving from out of state and, on the phone, sounded very eager to move. The couple walked in the house together, looked around, and after about 10 seconds the young woman turned and walked out. And that was that.

I never found out what the issue was, but it didn't matter, they simply were not moving in to that home. Even though I could keep the $200 in earnest money, winter was fast approaching and I spent the next two months trying to attract someone qualified. After reducing the rent amount and taking a beating from the extended vacancy, I made it a policy – I didn't care how much someone begged – they needed to have a friend or personal representative walk the property or we simply would not process their application.

Yard signs

In many markets, yard signs are a very important part of advertising vacant units. Yard signs should include the most important information, but don't make the mistake of cramming too much information on there. Remember, people are driving by at high speeds (and likely while texting on their phones). Make it easy for prospects to glean the vital information. Note that the toll-free number from your automated phone system is already in place.

FOR RENT

24 Hour Toll Free Number

877-555-4444

www.YourWebSite.com

Stop and Consider: In some markets, I would not place a yard sign on purpose because of the potential for vandalism and break-ins. There are companies that can place an active, cell-phone based alarm system in the property for about $30 per month with no contract if this is concern in your area.

Prescreening your Prospects and Fair Housing Law

Once the calls start coming in, the automated information line you set up through Grasshopper will answer many of the time-wasting, repetitious questions that used to suck your time. Sometimes, prospects will just press '0' and make no effort to listen to the recording. Unfortunately, that's part of the process. However, don't allow these people derail you from asking your necessary questions **before** you agree to schedule an appointment. Here is a list of questions that need to be asked. Feel free to adjust the wording to fit your style of speaking, but be careful not to violate Fair Housing Law.

- May I ask how quickly you're looking to move in to a new home?

  This is absolutely necessary. The last thing you want is to go through an entire showing only to find out that they want to rent the house four months down the road, when you need the house rented by the end of the current month.

- How many people will be in the household?

  Notice I asked how many "people," not how many adults or children. The wording here is key, and will keep you out of Fair Housing trouble. In general, two people per bedroom plus one person is a good guideline. A two-bedroom house, for example, would allow for no more than five people as a good rule of thumb (two people per bedroom, plus one person). I can't stress this enough, don't ever make decisions to rent based on the presence of children.

- What is your budget for housing?

  Even though someone may be calling on a specific house, don't assume that this is the amount they've budgeted for housing. I would generally pose the question, "So this house is currently priced at $895. Are you trying to stay under that amount or did you have a different budget you're working with?" I then explain further, "I ask this because I may have other units priced differently in case this house doesn't work for you."

Once I get answers to these questions, I will then answer any other questions they may have and schedule a showing. The next chapter will cover how to move forward when a prospect becomes an applicant.

The Power of Process

Chapter Eighteen

Resident Application Process

I don't own emotion, I rent.

- Jonathan Larson

Everyone has a story, and I do mean everyone. Some are interesting, perhaps comical, while others are simply heartbreaking. However compelling these stories might be, **none** of them should be a factor when selecting a qualified resident for your rental property. It's fine to listen to their story, but always defer to your application process when making a decision. Staying out of their personal business will be covered further in Part Four, but in terms of the "Process" in the PEB Model, it starts with the application itself. A sample, downloadable, Resident Application is available on our site at www.LandlordCoach.com/twiBook but your resident screening service should provide you one as well. Whatever you end up using for an application, I'd insist that you have your attorney look at it to ensure you're not violating any Fair Housing or ADA Laws by any questions you might ask.

Let's assume we have shown the property to a prospect, and they are ready to move forward. The next step for them is filling out an application. It's at this point you need to have a little bit of discipline and follow your process. As tempting as it might be to accept that lump sum of cash from the person standing in front of you and move them in today, you must resist the urge to do so. Yes, I've done this, and I've done it more than once. And no, hardly ever did it work out in my favor. You should consider the reason why this person is so desperate to move in. If they can't take the time to go through the application process, they would likely be a better customer for someone else.

> Stop and Consider: You are not in the social services business, and you do not owe it to **anyone** to fast-track (read: ignore) your application process simply to accommodate a complete stranger with a compelling sob story. Yes, I have heard just about every variation of the story of someone sleeping in their car, or having only enough money for rent and none for both food or a hotel room. You have a business to run and making decisions based on emotions is a recipe for disaster. Almost every time I hear a story like this from a Time-Weary Landlord, they all say nearly the same thing: "I knew I shouldn't have, but I just felt sorry for them."

> When people have kids, especially young ones, the temptation is even more difficult. If this is something you're going to struggle with, be honest with yourself up front. Hire someone else to do the showings who has had Fair Housing training, such as a Realtor. You can also consider a lockbox system such as Rently, which allows the residents to do self-showings. This removes you from the showing process entirely and allows you to be more objective. More information on the Rently lockbox service is located at www.rently.com.

Just understand the impact this will have on your ability to manage your rental property, or the impact it will have on that of your VA if you place someone in your property who is a disaster waiting to happen. Simply put, you don't owe it to anyone to put them in a home unless they are qualified.   To qualify our prospects, we direct them to the application process in the next section.

Online Application

After you show the property to the prospect and they agree to move forward, the prospect should be directed to your website where they will fill out the online application and pay the application fee. They will also need to provide you with a copy of the photo ID's for each applicant, as well as one month's worth of paystubs or other proof of income.

I recommend having your application only in digital form on your website so you don't have to worry about collecting paper applications from your prospects in person. This allows your VA to process them as soon as they come in. Online applications will also reduce the possibility of a prospective renter submitting an application after someone else has been accepted. This could otherwise lead to the perception of playing favorites and a Fair Housing claim "you didn't accept my application because I'm from Bangalore," for example.

Everything I explain to them is also written policy on my website. Here are some recommended practices to implement for your Application Process:

- I recommend a policy where the application itself does not hold the property for them. The only way to hold the property is to put a deposit down, call it Earnest Money or Hold Money, to hold the property based on the rent amount – 50% of one month's rent, for example. I tell the prospects they are in no way obligated to put Hold Money down during the application process. However, even if they are approved, someone else could step in front of them by submitting a completed application with Hold Money.

- The Hold Money becomes non-refundable once they have been approved. The Hold Money will be forfeited if they decide to walk away from the transaction. This keeps away the tire-kickers and people who will just waste your time. If they are denied, of course they get their Hold Money refunded immediately – mailed to the address of record. If an application has been processed, the application fee is never refunded.

- Consider in advance how many days Hold Money will secure the property for the applicant. Once someone has been approved and has put Hold Money down, I will apply that money to their security deposit. I establish a two-week timeline, or other date based on when they want to take possession. If residents don't take possession of the property, they forfeit their Hold Money and the property goes back on the market. Otherwise, you'll get residents who will delay taking possession indefinitely and cause you unnecessary vacancy expense.

- Make sure you get approved applicants to sign a Pre-Lease Commitment Sheet when they put down Hold Money; an example of this is available at www.LandlordCoach.com/twibook. The Pre-Lease Commitment Sheet indicates the date on which the future resident will take possession of the property, as well the utilities and other important information. This is for both you and the future resident, so there's no confusion as to the move-in date.

- Some landlords compile several prospect applications and select the best person of the lot. Doing it this way, in my opinion, is a bar-fight, and possibly a lawsuit, waiting to happen. Process the applications as they come in and either approve or deny based on screening criteria established and posted on your website. If they're approved, then proceed. If they're denied, then go to the next candidate in the order they came in.

- The application should ask all the specific questions to not only screen the residents, but to also help with the collections process if they should fall behind on their rent payments. I'm amazed at how many times I bring on a property from an owner only to find that the residents' lease has expired, and there's no application. If there is an application, there's seldom any helpful information to use in the collections process. Make sure you get all the information up front. Once the residents take possession, consider the possibility that you might never hear from them again.

- I suggest charging an application fee. This prevents people from submitting applications that aren't serious prospects. Call around and see what some other landlords and property managers in your area are charging and use the average. Some charge a flat application fee; others charge per adult applicant.

- Be sure you're processing *all* the adult occupants in the house. Exceptions to this rule might be an adult child who is in college and not earning an income, or an adult that does not have the mental capacity to enter into legal contracts.

Stop and Consider: An issue that you'll encounter fairly often is where one person will want to be listed on the lease, and the other person will not. Chances are the other person has some sort of checkered past that they are trying to hide, which is why the "clean" person wants to be on the lease by themselves. Politely explain that everyone needs to be listed on the lease so they all would have equal access to the property. Most people, at that point, will either concede and move forward or go away.

The screening process is not something to be taken lightly nor rushed through. I strongly recommend using National Tenant Network (NTN) www.ntnonline.com for resident screening. I have looked at many others and the main reason I prefer NTN is because their information is both timely and relevant. Consider the fact that if someone is in the middle of being evicted, their information may not show up on many data collection sites for a month or more *after the eviction has been settled!* This is craziness and certainly no way to make a sound business decision.

Declining Prospects

Declining prospects is part of the business. By placing someone in one of your properties that is not qualified, you are putting your vision at risk, and setting them up to fail. Make the decline process easy so you can delegate it to your VA. This highlights the importance of why you need a VA with exceptional people skills. Yes, it's important for them to be detail and task oriented, but not so much they forget you're still in the business of serving people.

The best approach is to contact the prospect directly and decline the application. Much like firing someone, don't keep them in limbo. You owe it to them to do it quickly and get it over with.

Don't just approve them because you want to avoid an awkward conversation only to say to yourself three months later, "How did I wind up with *these* people?"

Create a dialogue for your VA to use. It should go something like this:

> "Hello Mr./Mrs./Miss [Applicant's Last Name],
>
> This is Dave, the office assistant for ABC Rentals. Did I catch you at a bad time?

Wait for answer:

> "Ok great, (or) I'm very sorry this will only take a minute.
>
> I wanted to let you know that your application has been processed, and unfortunately, we are not able to approve you at this time. I don't have any of the details, but they will be mailed to your address of record. If you paid any hold money, it will be returned and sent to you in the same way you submitted it. Please have a wonderful day."
>
> There may be other dialogue beyond that, but with limited information, there really isn't much more that can be said. What is important, though, is that the Adverse Action letter goes out in the mail immediately, along with the return of their hold money. An Adverse Action letter is used to inform applicants that they have been denied when it involves using information from their credit report. Your resident screening service should be able to provide a sample Adverse Action letter. A sample can be downloaded by going to www.LandlordCoach.com/twiBook.

The Power of Process

Chapter Nineteen

Moving-In

A good friend will help you move, but a true friend will help you move a body.

- Steven J. Daniels, Author

Assuming you have prospects who are well-qualified, you would set a date for them to move in as indicated on the Pre-Lease Commitment Sheet. The move-in process sets the tone for your resident's experience right out of the gate with your company.

> Pre-Inspection – Make sure the house is move-in ready by performing a pre-inspection before you're in the presence of the new residents. This should be done at least one day before the move-in is scheduled just in case something was overlooked. Don't show up 20 minutes before the move-in is scheduled and think you're going to be able to correct anything that is wrong. If you're not a particularly detailed person, hire someone, such as a realtor, to do the inspection for you. This is something you really must pay close attention to because the move-in is such a critical time. Get this wrong, and you're

always playing from behind. Get this right, and you could have an advocate forever.

Move-in Gift Basket – You don't need to spend much money to show your new residents that you care about them. A small decorative basket or bucket filled with useful things to help them transition during their move is a nice touch. What types of items should go into the gift basket? Here are a few ideas: a shower curtain, a roll of toilet paper (since theirs is probably boxed up), and a coupon or gift card to a local restaurant. One property manager I know leaves a box of spaghetti noodles and a jar of pasta sauce with a note "Your first meal is on us!" These are all good ideas, just ensure their new home is ready to go, or this small gesture could backfire in a big way. The angry new resident barks, "Oh, you can give me a $5 Starbuck's gift card but you can't make sure my carpets are shampooed?" Fair point. Take care of the big details before tending to the small ones.

Move-In Packet – Your VA can put a move-in packet together for you to print off. It should be presented in a folder or large envelope containing a hard copy of the lease, instructions for contacting your office for issues or questions, plus information on local restaurants and attractions. Many apartment communities use move-in packets with great success.

Perform the Move-In Video – Make sure the resident understands why you're there shooting the video. Do the walk through with them first and encourage them to point things out on the video once you start. Sample videos are available to view at www.LandlordCoach.com/twiBook.

Call them – Many landlords take the approach of throwing the keys at their new residents and turning their phones off for fear of hearing from them. Have your VA set up a call to them at least once during the first week to make sure the transition to their new home has been smooth. If it hasn't, they should be asked if there is something your company can do to help. Any maintenance items missed during the move-in inspection should be addressed right away. Keep in mind they might be new to the area and need a referral to a dentist, a good chiropractor, or a trustworthy car repair shop. Allow your VA to do some research for them. It's for this reason I truly value my BNI networking group; I'm helping my resident by referring business to someone I know, like, and trust to take good care of my customer.

Videos

It's important to understand how truly valuable a well-executed move-in and move-out video can be to the overall experience of the residents. Not to mention helping your overall sanity. As mentioned earlier, several sample videos are available on www.LandlordCoach.com/twiBook for your review. Please note the particulars of how I go about shooting the video, as well as the specific narrative I do while performing the video. Practice this a few times before you do it in front of a new resident so you feel confident and comfortable.

Key points:

- Make sure the phone is held in the proper orientation. As a general rule, do not shoot vertical videos.
- Always start outside at the address number. State the address, if it's a move-in or move-out video, and the date including the year.

- Make sure you pan the room *slowly*. I had a few videos that were done by previous maintenance technicians that were done so fast it was difficult to identify anything useful, except for maybe a few comments here and there.
- Highlight the things in the room that are easy to miss such as cracks in windows, blinds, screens and similar items.
- If there is an issue with something that is your company's fault, don't try to hide it! This is the purpose of the video. Simply own the problem and say on the video, "The refrigerator needs a better cleaning, and we will take care of that right away." Trying to hide it on the video just makes you look dishonest. Own your mistakes and your residents will appreciate it.
- Keep in mind that the video feature on your phone is great, but you'll need a way of getting it off your phone and archived logically so you can find it later on when you'll need it. You can either connect to a desktop computer or upload these videos to the cloud via Dropbox or something similar. This can chew up an enormous amount of data, so you should probably do this when you're connected to WIFI. If you're going to save this to a desktop or laptop, you can plug in via USB and save it that way. Make sure you get it off your phone as soon as you can. If you drop or lose your phone, you've also lost your videos.
- When archiving and naming files, I recommend always using the same file format. For instance, "123 Main Street – June 1, 2016 – Move-In"
- Ideally, the residents will be present during the videos. It is always good if you can at least catch a glimpse of them when panning a room. However, I do all I can to make

sure I don't get their children in the video if I can help it. It's not necessary; and besides, it's just plain creepy.

- Capture the video in one continuous file if possible. Ensure you have enough capacity on your phone or video device when you're going to be recording. Saving memory space is another reason to make sure you get old videos off your phone as quickly as possible.

Back to Jack

Jack's business is starting to look completely different from just a few weeks ago. With his PM Software in place, he was up and running with his residents right away. He decided it made no sense to go back and enter in all the resident's transactions since he already had a good history of their accounts. Once Jack finds a good VA, he will have the VA input those data for him. He also got his Grasshopper phone system fully implemented and up and running, paying for only the calls that come in instead of opting for one of the volume packages. Jack took his wife's offer to record the calls since he realized people would much rather listen to her voice than his. In the future, he planned to have the VA take care of that too.

Jacks search for a VA has not been particularly easy. Working with one was a new endeavor and he wasn't entirely sure what questions to ask or what to look for. He's had to retrace his steps a few times to ask previously interviewed VAs other questions he'd later thought of. He laughed at the thought of hiring a VA to interview other VAs for him.

Eventually though, a simple Google search of "Virtual Assistants Property Management" lead him to the one he decided upon. He opted to go with a larger firm that would be able to answer his phone calls 24 hours a day and on the weekends. They seemed to be very well organized, and had worked with others in property management.

These VAs were used to managing properties, so they were already familiar with the types of calls that would come in from residents. Jack found this to be immediately helpful since, at first, he wasn't entirely sure what kind of help he needed. For $125 per month, they could handle many overnight calls that would come in and work with his approved maintenance vendors according to his parameters. He realized his process needed a little tweaking when the VA emergency dispatched one of his handyman vendors to a house with a clogged toilet that had two full bathrooms. Obviously, it would have been more of an emergency if there was only one toilet, but he wasn't upset. He knew things like this would come up, and had budgeted for it.

The additional cost for this infrastructure was nothing compared to the savings he was already realizing by getting plugged back in at work and resolving maintenance requests in a more timely manner. In fact, now that he was able to handle maintenance requests more efficiently, he was in a much better position to start collecting late fees due from his residents and not waiving them because he felt guilty. With the help of Sarah, his assigned VA, he was thinking of a process which would enable him to stay on top of collections and, without much effort, completely offset the cost of hiring her in the first place.

The Power of Process

Chapter Twenty

Collections

When it is a question of money, everybody is of the same religion.

- Voltaire

The collections function is where a good Virtual Assistant can be worth their weight in gold. Depending on your lease, you may choose to allow for a grace period for rent to be paid. Whatever the drop-dead day of the month their rent is due, on the first day rent is late, the collections process must start immediately. DO NOT WAIT! Even waiting one day to make that phone call, send that email, or mail that late-letter is one more day you will not have your money. Plus, this short-circuits the Process-Expectations-Behavior paradigm. Your behavior conveys to the residents that paying rent on time isn't important if you're not sending out "Late Notices" on a timely or consistent basis. How, then, can you expect to change your resident's behavior? Own it by having a solid process in place and a capable person to run it. By setting up a clear process, your VA will know what to do, and when to do it.

In the electronic age, I suggest you send out the first round of late notices via email, then follow up with a phone call, both of which should be done by your VA. You will want to set the feature on your email to request a "Read Receipt" so you know the resident received and read your email. The reason I send out emails at this stage is because sending out a physical letter is both time consuming and expensive. It's much easier to set up a form letter in your PM software, or do a simple copy-and-paste into your email, and hit "Send".

Plus, I have found that at least half of those notices we were sending out would cross in the mail and we would get the check the next day. Most people now get email on their phones. Followed up with a phone call, this is much more effective, efficient, and timely than mailing a letter.

Your timeline for collections may look something like this:

1st Day of the Month – Rent Due

3rd Day of the Month – Last day of Grace Period

4th Day of the Month – Send out Collection Emails / Phone calls

5th – 7th Day of the Month – Phone calls

8th Day of the Month – Mail Late Letters / Collection Emails / Phone calls

9th Day of the Month – Phone calls

10th Day of the Month – Mail Notice to Pay or Quit – Intent to Evict

11th Day of the Month – Phone calls

12th Day of the Month – Initiate court action – File eviction

It may look as though you're having your VA do a lot of phone calls, but this really isn't the case. Keep in mind there will be weekends and holidays during those first twelve days of the month. If a task lands on any non-work day, perform that activity on the next business day. For example, if the 1st is on a Friday and the last day of my grace period lands on a Sunday, the 3rd day of the month, I won't charge a late fee to anyone whose rent is in my drop box or mail box when I arrive to work Monday morning. I would assume that it was there on the 3rd even though I didn't get it until the 4th when I arrived at work. When it comes to late letters and other notices, move the task on your checklist to the next business day.

Rule No. 1: Never lose money.

Rule No. 2: Never forget rule No. 1.

- Warren Buffett

The Psychology of Money

Collections for many landlords is incredibly uncomfortable. In fact, whenever someone was looking to hire me as a property manager, chasing people down for money was nearly always in their top three reasons why they didn't want to manage the property themselves. For many people, talking about money in general is just plain uncomfortable. With that in mind, let's put a process in place that sets you up to win. Understanding what makes an effective collections process will do just that.

The most effective collections function is, in essence, a good sales function. Going one step further, great collections agents are really good salespeople at heart. If you think of the best salespeople, they aren't trying to convince you to buy something you don't need. They are solutions-based – getting to the bottom of what problems their product or service can solve for the person in front of them. The best salespeople are the ones who understand their client's needs and budget, as opposed to ones that simply launch into a torrent of features and benefits and rely on persuasion.

Imagine someone who is friendly and enjoys the challenge of helping people get their accounts squared away. Given limited funds, the collections person is selling the idea as to why residents should pay their rent *first* before they pay any other obligations.

Being friendly doesn't mean you're a pushover. You can be friendly yet firm at the same time. Remember, effective collections agents are actually great salespeople at heart. While they may love working with people and helping them, they aren't going to give away their product for free. With that in mind, a sample Late Notice-email from your VA might look something like this:

Dear [Resident],
DATE

We hope this finds you well. We wish we didn't have to send this to you, but as of today your account remains unpaid for this month. Unfortunately, a late fee has been posted and your total balance due is $[account balance pulled automatically from your Property Management software]. We hope to get this cleared up as soon as possible so you can avoid any additional fees being assessed to your account. Keep in mind you can pay online at our website at www.ABCRentals.com (some processing fees will apply).

We understand mistakes sometimes happen, but we do need to know when we can expect a payment from you. We look forward to getting this taken care of right away so you can continue to live comfortably in your home.

Kind Regards,

Your Name
P.O. Box XX
Anywhere, US

I realize for some of you this may be slathering on the syrup a little too thick, but remember you're selling them on the idea that using their limited funds to pay the rent is in their best interest versus using their money for other things. As the old saying goes, you catch many more flies with honey than you do with vinegar. Besides, if they don't respond to this notice, the rest of the collection function is soon to follow and the tonality of the letters will become more direct. Although, the tone of the phone calls should always remain upbeat, positive, and friendly.

Stop and Consider: While the collection process is something you may delegate to your VA, not all VAs may feel comfortable doing this. Because of this, it may not be the most effective use of their time. Unless this person has a strong background in solutions-based selling, or previous collections experience, I'd discourage you from having just anyone do this important function for you. Instead of a VA, you might want to consider hiring a professional collections agent to do this for you. Find out how they speak to customers on the phone, and make sure you would be able to audit the phone calls in case a negative customer experience is reported to you.

If you think you can take care of your own collection calls, I strongly suggest you reconsider. The whole point in developing this infrastructure is to take work off your plate. If you are doing this work now, with no intent of delegating it later, I would argue you're not valuing your time highly enough as a property owner, nor will it get you to the level of Time-Wealth we're trying to achieve.

Something else to consider here is the issue of compartmentalization. While *you* may be able to mentally separate the tasks of leasing agent, maintenance technician, office manager, and collections agent, it's very unlikely your tenant will be able to mentally separate you in those roles. The friendly "leasing agent" in you, who they met when they first saw the home, will be a stark contrast for them when you're assessing damages because their dog launched itself through the patio screen door. They will be angry because your kindness is being confused with stupidity, and their dog's actions are somehow your responsibility, or at least not their responsibility. However, if the system assesses the charge, and the collections person conveys how sorry they are that their dog did the damage, it is much easier to collect, and it leaves you out of the conversation entirely.

Collections Script

Whether you ultimately choose to keep the collections process for yourself or not, consider drawing up a script for your VA or collections agent to use when you're ready to turn it over. The spirit of the calls should be friendly, but not casual. Remember, your call is to solve a problem for your resident, not to drop the hammer on them.

VA: "Hi, Fred?"

Fred: "Yes, this is Fred."

VA: "Hi Fred, this is Mark from the leasing office [or your company name]. I wanted to speak with you about your account. Did I catch you at a bad time?" Asking permission to speak to them always lets them know that you respect their time.

> Note: If they say "No, it's not a good time," simply reply, "Okay, no worries; I just needed to inform you that your account is currently delinquent and it's accruing late fees. Please give me a call as soon as possible so we can talk about this further." Many times, given the context of the call, they will find at least a few minutes to discuss their account unless they are at work or in a situation where they simply cannot take the call. If they still say no, or hang up on you, well... you have your answer. At that point, you can proceed with the collections process.

If you get permission:

> Fred: "Yes, I've got a few minutes now."

> Note: Roughly half the time the resident will offer a date to pay their rent before you even have to ask. The other half are going to make you come out and ask.

VA: "Well, we were reviewing your account and we noticed your payment hasn't been received just yet. I'm sure it's an oversight, but unfortunately late fees have already been assessed. The balance as of right now is

$1,150." Do you have any idea of when we can expect that payment?"

At this point, the conversation can go in a few different directions. The most important thing to remember is you're there in that moment to help them. It's also important to listen, remain calm, and thoroughly document the conversation. This is where having a phone system that can record phone calls is invaluable. If your phone system has this ability, it will automatically tell inbound callers their phone call is being recorded. However, with outbound calls, the person initiating the phone call would have to inform the person of this. The tricky part is, in general, you'd need to initiate the call from the actual VOIP phone for outbound calls to be recorded. However, your VA or collections agent may offer the ability for calls to be recorded, so be aware of this if they will be making calls for you.

> Stop and Consider: Federal Law permits the recording of phone calls and in-person conversations with at least one party's consent (that one party would include you). However, as of this writing, some states require **both** parties to give consent. Those states being California, Connecticut, Florida, Maryland, Massachusetts, Montana, New Hampshire, Pennsylvania, Washington, and Illinois (although Illinois' Law was deemed unconstitutional in 2014, so good luck knowing what to do there).

> Here's an easy solution: Inform everyone you talk to that the call is being recorded.

"Hi, it's Mark from the leasing office, did I catch you at a good time? Great, I hope this finds you well. I need to inform you that I'm calling from a recorded line…" and then proceed with the rest of the call.

Having phone calls recorded holds everyone to a higher standard and all but eliminates the "but your assistant said this" nonsense which can drive you absolutely crazy. Before you get to the point of chasing imaginary butterflies around the room in a hospital gown, implement this sooner than later.

One thing you should be prepared for is the ubiquitous excuse, "Well, I've got all sorts of things broken here around the house. When are you going to come fix them?" Do not allow yourself to get distracted by this. Perpetual late-payers know this tactic and use it well and often. Give your VA the license to act so he can promise them, before the call is over, that he will address all their maintenance concerns and get someone dispatched.

Ramping up the Rhetoric

As the collections process continues, you will need to send out physical letters and give the residents notice of the delinquency. I'm treading on legal ground here that varies significantly in different areas, so be sure you know the laws in your area by consulting with an attorney. It would also be wise to familiarize yourself with the federal Fair Debt Collections Act to ensure everything you're doing is within the legal boundaries. Here's a sample letter with a more direct tone, which I would send out on Day 8 of our timeline.

Dear [Resident],
DATE

We hope this finds you well. We sent you a notification of your Past Due rent several days ago; as of today's date your account remains unpaid. Unfortunately, late fees continue to be assessed to your account and your total balance due is $[account balance pulled automatically from your PM software]. We had hoped to get this cleared up by now to avoid any additional fees being assessed to your account and further collection activity, which may include legal action. Keep in mind you can pay online at our website at www.ABCRentals.com (some processing fees will apply).

We understand that sometimes people fall behind on their bills, but we do need to know when we can expect payment from you. This is becoming serious. We look forward to getting this taken care of right away so you can continue to live comfortably in your home.

Kind Regards,

Your Name
ABC Rentals, LLC
P.O. Box XXX
Anywhere, US 99999

Depending on the laws in your area, you may have to send a notice to "Pay or Quit" or otherwise notify your resident of your intention to initiate legal action. I have always sent a "Notice of Intent to Evict", which I feel is anything but ambiguous as to what's going to happen next if they don't pay. If it progresses much beyond that, the next step in my collections timeline is to simply turn it over to my attorney to file for the eviction. There's only so much hand-holding you can do. Sometimes it's just best to cut your losses and move on.

Final Thoughts

There is a lot more we could cover on collections, such as what to do when you get a partial payment, or how far you let someone get behind before you pull the plug on them. There's really no right answer because every situation is different. However, if someone is a month behind, I seldom let them get much further than that. You have to remember trying to get caught up is almost impossible when someone is already living paycheck to paycheck. You could always set them up on a payment plan where you divide up what they owe over a six, eight, or twelve-week period. Sweeten the pot by agreeing to waive additional late fees if they stick with this plan and keep their future rent payments on time. Whatever you agree to, just make sure you have the fortitude to stick to your guns if they don't follow through.

The Power of Process

Chapter Twenty-One

Renewals and Move-Outs

**Excellence is a continuous process
and not an accident.**
                        **- A.P.J. Abdul Kalam,
                        11th President of India**

Renewal Process

With the help of your Property Management software, your VA is going to generate a monthly report on the 1st of each month as directed by your monthly checklist that you and he have collectively created. Let's say he notices on the report that a resident's lease is expiring in 90 days. Your VA emails you to ask if you want to renew this resident, pointing out their payment history and any notes in their register regarding communications with them. If the resident's payment history is good, and their communications show no reason to suggest that they are undesirable to work with, you respond back to your VA with the new, increased rent amount and lease terms. The VA prepares an email with the following sample script:

Dear {Resident's First Name},

We hope this finds you well. We at ABC Rentals, LLC want to thank you for being a valued client for the past 21 months. Roughly 90 days from now, your lease will be expiring and as a valued client, we wanted to reach out to you and make you aware of that. We know how much of a hassle it is to move and we would like to keep you as a customer, so we'd like to extend an offer for you to renew your lease.

Due to a rise in expenses, your rent will increase slightly. Your new lease amount will be $1,035, with your new lease term being 12 months from May 31st. This offer of renewal is good for 7 days from today. Due to changing market conditions, we retain the right to revoke this offer at any time up until the new lease is signed by you. Thank you for your understanding.

We will send the renewal lease in electronic form for you to review and sign at your earliest convenience. Thank you in advance for making this a priority.

We hope you find these terms agreeable to you, and look forward continuing to serve you as a client. We know you have many choices in rental housing; thank you for choosing us.

Best Regards,

Your Name

ABC Rentals, LLC

The VA sends the resident the above email and an electronic copy of their new, proposed lease, ready for their e-signature via DocuSign (www.Docusign.com). During this process, the VA will send gentle reminders every few days to both you and the resident, as appropriate, to prevent the renewal process from stalling out. If the resident does not renew, then no sooner than 60 days prior to their lease expiration, the VA will begin marketing the property, or earlier if they have already told you they're not renewing. The advertising on the property will continue until either one of two things happens: the resident renews their lease, or the property is rented to someone new.

Negotiating from Strength – Rent Increases

You always want to increase rent when renewing leases. Always! Even if it's only $5 or $10 per month, you never want the resident to get into the mindset of thinking that their current rent amount is set in stone. Even if they are the best tenants since Mary and Joseph rented the manger, I would suggest small increases each and every year.

Consider the alternative if you didn't increase the rent for three years, not noticing your margins are slipping. Then, after the third year, you notice a big increase in your insurance rates, and you need to increase the rent by $100 per month. Here's the reaction you would likely receive from your residents:

> "Wow! What a jerk my Landlord is! He is trying to screw us with a $100 increase in rent!"

Consider now the contrast if you'd been increasing the rent each year by only $20 per month. The difference in math is simple:

Year one renewal plus $20 per month = An additional $240 per year. Equating to $240 additional rent revenues, $240 cumulative profit increase from beginning of year.

Plus $20 per month the second year = An additional $240 per year on top of the first year. Equating to $480 additional rent revenues in year two, $720 cumulative revenue increase from beginning of year one.

Plus $20 per month the third year = An additional $240 per year on top of the first two years. Equating to $720 total rent increase in year three, $1,440 cumulative revenue increase from beginning of year one.

Total increase in rent revenues over three years = $1,440 extra income from beginning of year one.

Compare this to keeping the rent amount the same, until the $100 increase in year three:

Year one renewal – No increase.

Year two renewal – No increase.

Year three renewal, $100 per month = An additional $1,200 per year. Equating to $1,200 total rent increase.

Total increase in rent over three years = $1,200 extra income, from beginning of year one.

Not only have you upset your Residents, you've made $240 less money! When, not "if", but when, an increase in property taxes, insurance rates, HOA Dues or similar expense comes down the pipeline, you at least have some cushion, and any increase would be more palatable.

For those of you who are reluctant to the idea, remember one fundamental truth when balking at increasing the rents on your property:

Moving is a GIANT hassle!

Keep in mind, it is quite likely the emotional pain of moving is greater than the emotional pain of staying in the house they are in. As long as they've been treated fairly and the house works for them, all things being equal, a few dollars more per month will be less pain than the hassle and expense of finding and moving into a new place.

This is the process for residents you want to keep as customers. Next, we're going to review the process for letting go of the residents who would be better customers for someone else.

Non-Renewal of Leases

For the residents you don't want to keep, you will have your VA send a letter indicating their lease is not going to be renewed. I don't know this to be the case in every state, but I do know that generally landlords are not obligated to renew leases to their residents in most areas. I suspect in areas that are less landlord-friendly, this may not be the case. If so, please be sure you're consulting with an attorney before making the decision not to renew, or sending out any sort of letter.

Here is an example of a letter I'd have my VA send out to residents we do not wish to renew:

Dear {Resident's First Name},

> We hope this finds you well. We want to thank you for being a valued client for the past 21 months. Roughly 90 days from now, your lease will be expiring and we wanted to reach out to you and make sure you were aware of that. We know how much of a hassle it is to move, and we wanted to give you as much advanced notice as possible so you can make arrangements for your coming move into your new home.
>
> We will send a move-out checklist in a separate email so we can help ensure a smooth transition for your move. This will also include some helpful tips for packing and things you may not have considered since moving is not something one does very often.
>
> We look forward to a smooth transition; please let us know if we can assist you in any way.
>
> Best Regards,
>
> ABC Rentals, LLC

There is no talk of renewal, nor is there any discussion as to why they are not being renewed. Renewals should *not* be automatic. If you're dealing with a less-than-desirable resident, stop dealing with the aggravation and find someone new. If this property is particularly difficult to rent, then you may want to consider if this is even a property worth keeping in your real estate portfolio.

You may be wondering why we're sending out renewal notices 90 days prior to the lease expiration. The renewal process should start in your office 120 days out. The reason for this has to do with one of our core rules:

Always Negotiate from a Position of Strength

Too often property owners get caught unaware of a renter who – in an expired, month-to-month lease – notifies you they are moving when it's a bad time of year to fill vacancies. Most markets have a time of year when it is most desirable to lease properties. In most Midwest markets, for example, the rental season is April through June. College campus markets however, may start as early as the middle of the first semester for the following academic year. It's all relative to your location and customer base.

Regardless of when your prime leasing season lands, qualified renters are more difficult to come by when you're outside of that period. You'll want to identify the prime leasing season in your area, and adjust your leases to those months. Have your VA monitor this through your property management software well in advance of the lease expiration dates. I recommend no less than 90 days, but adjust accordingly to your market.

Security Deposits

Security deposit returns are contested in courts all over the country. You're going to need an attorney who knows the laws in your particular area, especially because laws change from time to time. Hire an expert who stays on top of the changes so you stay compliant.

Fortunately, in most states, the law is straightforward. Based on my research, the laws vary from 30 to 60 days in which the security deposit or an itemization must be returned to the resident after the lease terminates. There are grey areas as to how a local judge might interpret different circumstances, so be sure to hire an attorney that is familiar with that particular court should that be necessary.

For example, say you live in a state that requires the security deposit to be returned within 30 days. You have a lease that terminates on June 30th, but the resident moves out early, provides a forwarding address, and gives you keys on June 10th. When does the clock start on returning the deposit within the 30 days? June 10th or June 30th? Some would argue the former, and others the latter. This is why it's important to have an attorney who works specifically in the field of landlord-tenant law. You may have an attorney already, but if their specialty is in some other field of law, like patents and trademarks, they may not be up on the nuances of the laws in situations like this.

Move Out Video

Just like the move-in video, the move-out video is crucial to helping you make sound decisions when it comes to the return of the security deposit. The move-out video is much more powerful when it can be compared in context to the move-in video. It shows you care about documentation and making fair decisions when you film these videos in the presence of the residents. You shouldn't be approaching the return of the deposit as "what can we charge the residents," but rather, "what can we do to give them back as much as possible?"

Some landlords choose to make a list of charges, or liquidated damages, which is part of the lease for certain things the landlord must do. Examples might be $5 per nail hole, or $3 per light bulb, etc. I don't think these are bad ideas, but I've found it to be a little more cumbersome to charge specific dollar amounts for things that are listed on the lease such as lightbulbs or counting nail holes.

I found it to be easier to estimate the hours it will take to do the necessary repairs, and what it would cost to get the property back in shape, excluding normal wear and tear. It's the "normal wear and tear" exception that gets dicey. Here's the standard I use for normal wear and tear. Let's say I lived in a house that I own, and moved out of. I got it professionally cleaned, carpets included, but the walls were scuffed up just from normal living. No crayon marks or anything like that, but from hanging photos on the walls and so forth. The walls will most certainly need to be painted, or at least touched up after my normal use of the property. That would be normal wear and tear.

"We left it cleaner than we found it!"

Nothing is more frustrating than hearing those words uttered from a past resident who moved out and left the place a mess. The best thing you can do is base your security deposit decisions on a good inspection, reviewing the move-in video compared to the move-out video, documenting everything with photos, and simply be fair.

Jack – Taking Charge

Jack has been working feverishly on his business the last few months. He's got a very clear vision as to what he wants his business to look like. Although he's had to adjust some things along the way, he's well on his way to getting there.

One of the things he realized is that the CPA he initially chose was not a good fit for him. She was very smart and technically proficient, but she was very slow to respond to his emails. On top of that, Jack was coming up to the end of one of his trial periods for PM software he was considering and he'd spent two weeks trying to get on her calendar. It wasn't tax-time, so he just got the feeling that she already had too many clients to handle. Jack had his VA draft a nicely-worded, three-sentence email:

> Subject: Change of Direction
>
> Hello Jessica,
>
> Jack wanted me to thank you for the time you've spent considering taking him on as a client. With his business expanding as rapidly as it is, he has decided to go in a different direction with his accounting needs.
>
> We wish you all the best in your future endeavors.
>
> Warm Regards,
>
> Sarah – Assistant to Jack Smith

Instead of adjusting the verbiage and removing her name from the signature line, Jack chose to leave the email exactly as it was and allowed Sarah to send it on his behalf. It allowed him to enjoy a little bit of a power-trip but still be very nice about taking charge of his business.

Jack's second choice of CPAs seems to be faring much better. Jack is dealing with a professional who values her time as much as she values his. While a little more expensive, the overall costs of using this CPA are likely to be lower since Jack is forced to be organized in his thoughts before calling or sending her an email.

Jack's use of his VA started out with simple emails and has gone on to much more than Jack had ever envisioned. At his job, there were a few office workers on staff, but Jack didn't have anyone to assist him with his daily tasks. He wasn't used to directing someone else's time, so it took some adjustment. Once he had some successes with the lower end tasks he had Sarah handling, he had the itch to venture into other areas. Soon, Sarah was preparing leases for his new and renewing residents.

Jack was beginning to see his efforts paying off. He wasn't quite ready for his business to take the next step, but he could see it in the future. The not-too-distant future.

Part III – Managing Expectations

Chapter Twenty-Two

Laying the Groundwork

**Expectations are a form of first-class truth:
If people believe it, it's true.**
- Bill Gates

Up to this point we have spent much of our time building the framework upon which your processes will operate. We've also spent considerable effort developing processes in your real estate business, taking the time to put them in place. A critical piece to the PEB Model is the Expectations portion, which is addressed in this section of the book.

Clear expectations are critical to having effective relationships with your residents. Not only does it convey what you expect from them, but also what they can expect from you. This is the essence of any good contract, and is the approach you should take when putting together your lease.

From Process to Setting Expectations

We have talked in great detail about the framework and processes your real estate business will run on. You may be wondering why I waited so long in the book to bring up the lease. After all, this is a book about managing your rental properties more effectively right? Remember, to get the behavior we want from our residents, we must follow the Process-Expectations-Behavior model, *in that order*. Once they know the process, the lease lays out the expectations.

I opted not to provide a sample lease for this section simply because I know it would be downloaded and passed around like the flu, disregarding what you have built up to this point and defeating the entire purpose of getting you a lease that actually works for *you*. Take the time to have an attorney draft a lease addressing the risks that are important to you, and is in alignment with the infrastructure and processes you've developed. As much as I want to get into the weeds here on all the different topics in a lease, I have to be careful about offering what could be interpreted as legal advice. I'm not an attorney; that's why you need one of your own.

When you set up a meeting with your attorney, make the best use of your time by giving her some context for your meeting. If you just call and say you need a lease, your attorney has no knowledge of the framework you've created nor your vision for the future. You end up wasting a lot of time. On the other end of the spectrum, if you want her to check your seven-page Frankenstein that you've crafted by piecing together leases from all over the internet, you're going to wind up with the same problem.

Use your attorney to check for the legality and enforceability of your lease, not sorting through an array of mismatched paragraphs, one possibly contradicting the others. This is far too time-consuming and not a good use of your attorney's time, not to mention completely aggravating for someone on your team you want to keep happy. My advice is to create an outline of a lease and give her a basis for what you want it to say. State your concerns in a bullet point format, and question if there is a legal, and enforceable, manner in which to address them.

Stop and Consider: I've mentioned a few times that your lease should match your infrastructure, processes, and risk tolerance. Let me offer an example as to what I mean by that. Nearly every lease I've ever come across addresses late fees, and they are all charged in different ways. Some charge $5 or $10 per day. Some charge late fees until the day the rent is received, and others will charge the late fee based on the date it was postmarked (assuming it was mailed). Still others may charge $40 on the 5th of the month, then another $40 on the 10th, then $10 per day after that, or some other variation.

We'll talk more specifics on late fees later on, but for the purpose of this example, consider how you are set up to enforce and collect on them. Think through the logistics of specifically **how** you will be receiving the rent. If you are receiving it in the mail, will you be able to check the mail each and every day? If you're not able to commit to that, then charging a "per day" late fee isn't going to work well for you. It's the same issue if you have a drop box. If you don't plan to charge a daily late fee, but will charge it on specific days, you must ensure that you or your assistant will be able to check your mail on those specific days. You also need to figure how you will be entering the payments, otherwise you are going to make a lot of your good residents upset when your VA is contacting them about rent that's already been paid.

The Basics

The opening paragraph of the lease is fairly straightforward and addresses all the basics, such as the parties to the transaction, the date the lease is signed, the property address, and so forth. It will also have the effective dates of the lease, when it begins and when it ends, and what time it ends. Consider having your attorney use language that allows for a time such as 12 noon, or 4pm as an expiration time as opposed to midnight. This is so you can be clear in your expectations regarding when the property needs to be vacated. The more clarity you have in conveying your expectations, the less chance you will be disappointed in the resulting behaviors you experience. This will be a common theme in this section. Be specific and, when possible, use basic language a 5-year old would understand.

There are different schools of thought on the subject, but I've always preferred having a Master Tenant identified on the lease. The reason is because it's much simpler to go to one person for everything (payments, maintenance, lease violations, etc.) instead of chasing around three, or five. This would be especially important for those tenancies where you have, for instance, four people sharing a home and splitting the rent. It's common in situations such as this that the tenants each split the rent and pay their portion of the rent individually. However, the last thing you want to do is to have to chase down four separate rents from one property. I have always had a Master Tenant identified, but still listed the other occupants so they could be held liable for non-payment in case the Master Tenant flakes out and becomes incommunicative. Get with your attorney on how to word this, the enforceability on this, how to declare and identify a Master Tenant on the Lease Agreement, and if it makes sense for you.

Rent Amount

The rent amount should be both spelled out and written in numerical form. It should also be very clear as to when the rent is due, which is nearly always the first of the month. Some people choose to match the monthly rent payment to the day of the month when the residents first took possession. For example, if they moved in on the 12th of the month, the rent in subsequent months is due on the 12th. Maybe they didn't know how to calculate prorated rent, but I've never understood the reason for doing this. It's easier to always have the rent due on the first of the month. If you don't know how to calculate prorated rent, your PM software will do that for you. However, it's extremely easy to calculate manually as shown below, for example:

Rent Amount: $3,000
Move in day: 12th
Total Days in the month: 31

The math goes like this:
Rent amount divided by 30* equals rent charge per day
$3,000 / 30 = $100 per day rent charge

Total days in the month less the date of move-in equals the total days in possession:
31 days in the month less 12th move in day = 19 days in possession

Per day charge times days in possession equals prorated rent:
$100 per day x 19 days in possession = $1,900 owed for 19 days

The normal rent of $3,000 would then be due the first of the next month.
*(30 days is the standard used in the industry, regardless of the number of days in the actual month)

Grace Period

Whether you choose to have a grace period or not, make sure it is very clear on which day the late fee will be charged as I can guarantee any ambiguous language will be taken advantage of to the fullest extent. Language might look like:

> "Rent is due on the 1st and shall be considered late if received on or after the 4th calendar day of the month."

Your attorney will know the best language to put in your lease. Just make sure the verbiage is easy to understand so there's no confusion.

You're not required to provide a grace period for your renters. I prefer to offer one to make life a little easier on the resident without giving away the store. Providing a grace period gives the perception that you're not using late fees as a club with which to beat your residents. If you charge a $100 late fee for being one day late on rent, your resident is likely going to hold you to the same standard any time something breaks in one of your properties and you're not able to get someone to attend to it right away.

All that aside, late fees can become a substantial source of revenue in your real estate business. Here's where having a VA can really help you stick to your guns on late fees. Remember, the *system* charges the late fees, not you, not your VA. The expectation is that they pay the rent on time, and they agreed to that when they signed the lease.

You can give your VA or collections person some flexibility though, if it's warranted. If you are going to give them the authority, he can offer a one-time courtesy waiver of a late fee. Be sure it is well-documented by making a note in the resident register. After that, you simply MUST charge the late fees or you're opening the door to never getting your rent on time.

Late Fees

Some landlords go completely crazy with their late fees. I'm not here to judge you if you want to charge $150 per day in late fees for your $500 per month apartment. However, you must consider two things: 1) Are you late fees enforceable, and 2) Are they reasonable (and therefore collectible).

Concerning the first of the two, if you were to take this person to court, what would the court allow? Your attorney will know what the courts allow in terms of late fees. This is one section in your lease you will want to make sure is enforceable.

Second, your late fees should be stiff enough so they hurt, but not so stiff that they become uncollectible. You can put in the lease that late fees are a thousand dollars per day, but are they reasonable and collectible? Unless you're renting to a sultan, I'd say probably not. If you charge late fees that are disproportionately high, you're going to end up with angry residents and ultimately doing fee reversals or making concessions, which at some point, gets you involved. This defeats the very purpose of having a late policy and a VA to manage it for you. Late fees must be enforced consistently; to do so they must be reasonable.

If you're going to charge daily late fees, think through the steps of how they are going to be enforced. Logistically, this can become a hassle if you're going to rely on the resident to mail their rent to a mailbox you likely won't check every day. If you charge $5 per day as a late fee, for example, you'd often wind up contacting residents to collect on balances so small it's often not worth the effort. This is much less of an issue, obviously, if they pay their rent to you online since crediting to their account is instantaneous. Another way to charge late fees is to post them after a certain day, say $50 on the 4th, and another $50 on the 8th. You could then charge daily late fees if the rent continues to be unpaid.

Chapter Twenty-Three

Emotional Topics

The single biggest problem in communication is the illusion that it has taken place.

- George Bernard Shaw

Jack has been hard at work building his business, busier than ever actually. He wouldn't exactly describe it as horrible; in fact, it's been the exact opposite. Compared to his pre-infrastructure days as a Time-Weary Landlord, he's very much enjoying seeing all his infrastructure and processes in action. When a little tweaking is necessary, he works with his VA to close the gaps. On the 15th of every month, his VA, Sarah, holds a video conference with Jack using Zoom (https://zoom.us) to go over any developments which have come up over the previous month. Things that need to be addressed, recurring questions that should be answered and added to the FAQ or SOP, and checklist items that may need to be altered are all discussed.

There are occasions that come up where Jack feels a change to his lease might be warranted. He has his VA keep a list of things to discuss with his attorney the next time he sees him. He's called on several, deciding on a young guy recommended to him by his CPA. He really seems to know his way around contract law and landlord-tenant cases. He's reviewed Jack's lease once already and uncovered several important weaknesses concerning the security deposit and a few other key areas. The few hundred dollars Jack spent was well worth the potentially thousands of dollars he could have lost by his poorly-worded lease. A lease, admittedly, Jack downloaded from some website he can't even remember.

He's discovered one key thing about his lease that he hadn't expected. Through his lease, Jack communicates his expectations to his residents. This is something he'd never given much thought to before. While it might sound overly simplistic, this slight shift in paradigm brought him from using his lease as a weapon, to that of tool for communication. This change in thought process has had a profound positive effect on his relationships with his new residents.

Security Deposit

This topic could be the subject of an entire book on its own. Unfortunately, security deposits are confusing because in some areas there are specific laws on the books and in others it's the Wild West. If you want to see someone's emotions come into play about a previous landlord, just mention "security deposit" and watch their blood pressure rise. This is because, regardless where you live, the security deposit is the source of many complaints among past residents.

Don't set your residents up to fail. The return of the security deposit should be specifically addressed on the lease so there is no confusion as to what will cause deductions. These expectations must also be in alignment with what is allowed by law. You MUST consult an attorney about this. There are simply too many places for you to go wrong, and the return of the security deposit can hurt you badly if you're not paying attention.

For example, verbiage in the security deposit section should stipulate what constitutes surrender of the premises that is in alignment with your local laws. The date of surrender is important because, in most areas, it starts the clock for when the security deposit needs to be returned to the resident. According to my research, some states require the return of the security deposit as soon as ten days after the landlord has possession and there are no deductions. Other states, allow as much as 60 days. Regardless of where you live, if you fail to return the deposit or give the former resident an itemization of the charges, you are not going to like the outcome. No matter the actual damages, miss that deadline and you would likely have to return the deposit in full without any ability to collect on any damages after the fact. In some areas, if you mess this up, you may have to return up to three times the amount of the deposit!

There are states that mandate the payment of interest, put a limit on how much of a deposit you can collect, and laws requiring the security deposit be maintained in a separate bank account that is reviewable by the resident on demand. These laws vary widely, so, bottom line:

Do not rely on a lease downloaded from the internet… Hire an attorney!

I could give you many ideas about what to put in the security deposit section of your lease, however, the laws of your state may dictate what you can charge to your residents and what you cannot. Get an attorney, and let him navigate that for you.

Here are some questions to ask your attorney:

- Can I stipulate the residents must have a professional cleaning or carpet cleaning performed?
- Can I charge $150, for example, if a pet ever occupies the property during the term of the lease?

- Can I stipulate the security deposit shall not be used to cover the last month's rent?
- What actions on the tenant's part dictates when the clock starts for the security deposit to be returned?

Maintenance and Repair

There are a lot of topics that get your residents fired up, not the least of which is how maintenance and repairs are handled. Have your attorney craft this section and be as detailed as possible. State the expectations for both you and the residents and detail who is responsible for what. It should also explain who will pay for such repairs, and if they are not performed, what rate shall be charged for performing such actions, say $75 per hour, or the actual cost of the repair. This is especially important for damages caused by the resident's misuse or neglect.

Some landlords expect their residents to pay for everything, and I do mean everything. Whether this approach is something for you to adopt is not for me to judge, but I will caution you here. There are a lot of things you might be prohibited by law to place on the residents. Generally, you can task the resident for maintaining the property in good and sanitary condition and repair, including things such as the following:

- Keeping the lawn mowed, trimmed, and free from debris
- Keeping the sidewalk free from ice and snow
- Maintaining and weeding the landscaping and shrubbery
- Replacement of lightbulbs, water filters, and furnace filters
- Replacement of salt in the water softener tank as it is used

You should be able to place the financial burden back on the resident for having to take care of repairs caused by their misuse or neglect. You can be specific here if you like, but your attorney will know the best way to address this.

> Stop and Consider: Consider how you will handle things that happen to the property by a third party while the resident is in possession of the unit. This would include situations such as break-ins or vandalism. You might want to require that if criminal activity occurs on your property causing damage, you need to be notified within 24 hours and the residents must file a police report. Failure to do this could result in such damages being charged to the resident.
>
> Requiring a police report makes sense because filing a false police report is a crime. For the resident that kicks in the front door because they lost their key or got into an argument with their roommate, they would likely think twice before telling you someone broke in if you're going to require them to file a police report within 24 hours. What usually happens is they don't say anything at all, and just piece the door frame back together with staples and glitter glue. It's hardly a durable repair, but that's what they'll sometimes do in hopes you won't notice on an inspection.

Remember, this is about conveying expectations to your resident. There are many items that you can include in this section. Here are some other ideas:

- Require residents to report maintenance items in a timely manner. Failing to report maintenance that causes further damage shall be charged to the resident.
- Charge the resident a trip charge in the event that a prearranged inspection, maintenance, showing, or other

visit where you or a vendor is denied access. This can be due to the resident changing locks, having unsecured animals, locked screen doors, or is otherwise preventing access to the property.

- Detail the process of communicating maintenance requests, whether in writing, email, phone call, text message, or through a form on your website. As mentioned earlier, keep it simple. Don't offer more than just a few options or you'll drive your VA crazy trying to manage all the different communication sources.
- Detail the process of communicating emergency maintenance requests, and what constitutes an emergency. Consider making specific requirements such as "heating calls when the temperature is below 55 degrees or cooling calls when above 79 degrees", perhaps in combination with broad statements such as items related to "Habitability, Safety, or Security".
- Charge residents a fee for initiating emergency maintenance calls for things that are non-emergencies. You can choose to exercise discretion on how and when this is charged, but it's good to have in your lease to prevent abuse of your emergency number.
- Include a statement holding the landlord harmless from any loss that might be suffered by the resident for any improper functioning of the mechanical, structural, electrical, or plumbing systems. It's a good idea to reiterate that renter's insurance shall be required so they are protected from such perils.
- Declare that the resident shall be responsible for any damage to the property that occurs from the use of their own appliances.

Pets / Service Animals

Much can be said about either allowing or not allowing pets in your rental unit. To most people, pets are members of the family. By allowing pets in your unit, you open yourself up to a significantly larger pool of residents. If you do allow your residents to have pets, there are numerous things to consider. First, what kinds of pets should you allow? Most people think of dogs and cats, but residents' pets will run the gamut from spiders, snakes, rabbits, ferrets, chickens, lizards, frogs, birds, turtles, hamsters, mice, rats, pigs, fish, and crickets... just to name a few. No, you don't have to allow these sorts of pets, but you should be specific in terms of what you **will** allow.

Probably the easiest way to categorize pets is by dog, cat, cage, and aquarium tank. This way you can allow two pets, for example, which could be any combination of dog/cat/caged animal/aquarium tank animal. It would be ridiculous, for example, to charge someone by "number of goldfish", if they had four in one aquarium tank. One fish tank and one cat would be the better way to manage this. Specifically prohibiting anything that is not a dog, cat, bird, hamster, or fish, and only allowing other types of animals on a case by case basis, will help keep you out of the exotic-animal business.

Second, what fees do you charge? Some landlords I know go nuts with this, charging a non-refundable pet fee, in addition to monthly pet rent, as much as an additional $100 per pet per month. This is something you need to be careful with because you can easily price an otherwise good resident out of your housing or force your residents to be dishonest by not disclosing they own a pet. Less than scrupulous residents will identify their pet as a "therapy animal", in which case you are specifically prohibited by federal law from charging a pet fee.

If you are going to allow aquarium tanks, with fish as opposed to tanks used for hamsters, you should limit their size to being under a certain number of gallons, say 10 or 15 gallons. Consider the damage that could happen from a 100-gallon tank if that much water leaked out at one time. More water equals more potential damage. Risks for larger tanks can be mitigated with additional insurance, so talk to your insurance agent about how to offset that risk. For caged animals, like birds, you can treat them the same as aquarium tanks where you just limit the number of cages versus the number of animals.

> Stop and Consider: Service animals are NOT pets, and only under very special circumstances can you exclude them. Furthermore, you cannot charge a "pet fee" or "pet rent" for them. This is considered making a reasonable accommodation for someone with a disability. If you're not sure about the nuances in the American's with Disabilities Act (ADA), please take the time to educate yourself and be sure to contact an attorney who is familiar with this aspect of the law.

One final thing to consider is if you do charge pet rent, stipulate that the fee will stay for the entire term of the lease. This can drive you bananas when you get residents asking to remove a pet fee when you've got everything else going on. I suggest you put a clause in the pet section that stipulates such fees shall remain in place during the entire term of the lease, even if the pets no longer remain at the property.

Stop and Consider: Are you feeling overwhelmed? I get it, this part of the book might feel as if it's starting to drag. Plus, it can become overwhelming as your own ideas for process and expectations start multiplying like Catholic rabbits. Keep on it though. Write your ideas down and keep your foot on the gas. I promise, it will pay off once you're in control of your calendar.   If you need help or get stuck, reach out at www.LandlordCoach.com

Managing Expectations

Chapter Twenty-Four

The Fine Details

We forget the little things, so it's no wonder some of us screw up the big things.

- Neil Cavuto

There are numerous other details that make a huge impact when setting expectations with your residents. In the previous chapter, we covered the significant matters in your lease agreement. In this chapter, we go through smaller details that can have a major impact on the behavior you will allow to be acceptable.

Keep in mind this is not an exhaustive list. As you continue to educate yourself, you may find best practices and other tips along the way that would dovetail nicely with your infrastructure and processes. Be sure you don't make any changes to your lease without first consulting your attorney, and make certain that it doesn't contradict any other expectations you may have communicated in the form of your lease, FAQ, or SOP.

Manner of Payment

You'll want to indicate to your residents how and where you want them to pay the rent. This is where you'll list the address of your drop box, your mailing address, or the address of the lockbox service from your bank, should you decide to use one. If you're able to accept online payments, be sure to list your web address.

I know it may sound a bit odd, but consider making it a policy to not allow for money orders to be sent through the mail. It becomes a giant headache when you get residents claiming they mailed their rent in the form of a money order. Assuming that it was mailed, the efforts of getting money orders tracked and refunded from Walmart or a convenience store is about as productive as swatting gnats with a tennis racket.

Application of Payments

This section of the lease points out how money is applied as it comes in. Prioritizing payments prevents residents from ignoring charges to their account and letting them linger. A suggestion might be to apply payments first to unpaid security deposit, then damages, then late fees, then delinquent rent, then the current month's rent.

Applying payments this way prevents someone from falling behind on rent, ignoring late fees, and trying to pay the current month's rent. Notice that it will also force people to pay their balances in full each month or they can be subject to late fees.

Take this example:

Resident charged for lockout: $100 $100 Balance

Resident charged rent: $1,800 $1,900 Balance

Resident pays $1,800:   ($1,800) $100 Balance

In this example, the $100 that is owed is not from the lockout, but rather $100 in unpaid rent. Therefore, according to the terms of the lease, a late fee could be charged. It's for this reason there must be in place a solid process to notify the residents of charges to their accounts that they may not otherwise realize.

Forfeiture of First Rental Payment

The applicant commits to the property, they are qualified, you've established a move-in date and time, and everything is ready to go. They have even met with you the day before to sign the lease, paid $1,600 for the rent and balance of the deposit, and confirmed the move-in time for the following day. A few hours in advance of the move-in, you call to confirm, but the call goes straight to voicemail.

The move-in time comes and goes, and you start to get a bit worried. Your calls and texts go unanswered. Finding this all highly unusual, you're not sure if you should be concerned for their safety, or angry that they are forgetting your appointment for today. Or perhaps, they forgot entirely?

You never hear from these would-be residents. Your calls go unanswered; they don't call you back. You take the next week of silence as a hint that they don't want the property, so you put it back on the market and start the leasing process all over again. Several weeks go by and you find new residents, screen them, and move them into the home. While odd, you don't give much more thought about the original people. Until of course, they call two months later. Demanding a full-refund of their money. Huh? Are they for real?

The whole point of this story is to find out what would likely be enforceable if the residents sign the lease and ultimately fail to take possession. While rare, this does happen. Just make sure you get enough earnest money early on in the process to help reduce the likelihood of this happening. Also, have your attorney research the law in your area to allow you to keep the earnest money if they walk away from the transaction. This verbiage should also align with what is on your Pre-Lease Commitment Agreement.

Required Utilities

Be sure to list all the utilities required to maintain the habitability of the dwelling. This should include things like natural gas, water, electric, sewer, and trash – assuming all those things are billed separately – and should be paid by the occupant. If you have a rural property that has an LP gas or oil tank, that tank should be topped off prior to the resident's possession so you can ensure it's the same level when you get the property back. If not, they should be charged for the difference. Don't neglect this crucial step as this could cost you hundreds of dollars if you're not paying attention.

In warmer times of the year, it may not make sense to require gas services to be turned on if the only gas appliance is the furnace, but you should still require this up front. The last thing you want is to have the resident avoid paying a gas bill by heating the home with space heaters or the electric oven in the kitchen. Some utility companies require residents to have a copy of the lease to activate services. If that's the case, have the residents sign the lease, give them a copy, then provide them keys once they have confirmation numbers showing services have been activated. Requiring residents to provide proof of activation is a good policy.

There are some utility companies that offer an Automatic Turn-On Agreement if the utilities are shut off for non-payment or if the resident shuts them off. This might be a good idea if you're in a climate where the pipes can freeze, or you are concerned that sump pumps will fail if power gets shut off. Keep in mind, if the residents get their gas or electric shut off and you have an Automatic Turn-on Agreement in place, you might get a notification that the utilities have been switched to your name, but I wouldn't bet on it. Usually the first indication that the utilities have been switched over to you is when you receive a bill. I don't know about you, but the thought of getting a bill for several hundred dollars of someone else's utilities is not so cool.

If you do end up paying for your resident's utilities, have a process in place to notify them immediately and that you've assessed a fee for paying their bill. $75 per utility bill, for example. You can charge whatever you want, but I recommend that it be relatively stiff because of the added risk you are taking on. I would not, ***under any circumstances,*** offer to put utilities in your name and charge a fee as an additional source of revenue. The risk of paying someone else's utilities and having them reimburse you, regardless of the fee you charge, is simply too great. If they can't afford to pay their utilities, they surely aren't going to be able to afford your fees on top of them.

Once the utility bill is charged, plus the utility fee, to the resident's register, a notification should be sent immediately via email, letter, and phone.

A sample letter follows:

> Dear [Resident First and Last Name],
>
> We realize that this may be an oversight, but unfortunately, we just received an electric bill for the dates 1/1 to 1/31 in the amount of $275.25. According to the lease, this is a required utility and you are to arrange and pay for all required utilities. We will require payment of this immediately, plus the utility fee of $75, the total amount due is $350.25.
>
> Thank you in advance for your timely attention to paying this balance, as well as making arrangements for getting this utility back in your name.
>
> Best Regards,
>
> [Name of Virtual Assistant]
>
> ABC Rentals, LLC

Early Termination Clause

You might think giving the residents a built-in lifeboat to get out of their lease is a bad idea, but hear me out. While it's not something you must offer, it can help minimize vacancy expense. Here's why: If someone is going to leave, they are going to leave. Short of sitting out front of the property with a shotgun, there's not much you can do about it. People take new jobs, buy homes, and experience other exceptional circumstances causing them to move. Including a termination clause in your lease at least provides some protection when people want to get out of their lease early.

If you're going to place this clause in your lease, I suggest requiring at least 60-days' notice prior to the anticipated date of vacancy. Charge a termination fee equaling two-months' rent, and specifically reference the rent amount separately. For example, if the rent amount is $1,100 per month, make the termination fee $2,200 as opposed to referencing "Two month's rent as a termination fee". I find it makes it less confusing for the residents.

In addition to the termination fee, the resident should also be required to pay the rent as usual for the last two months that they are in possession of the property. I suggest that you make this rent un-prorated, just in case someone gives you notice mid-month so you don't wind up losing out of part of a month's rent. For instance, if someone gives you notice on October 12th, they would have to pay rent for the entire month of November and December, instead of only paying rent through December 11th. You should also require the resident to maintain the utilities during this time as well.

Be aware that residents may ask you if it's okay to forfeit their security deposit in lieu of paying the termination fee. I strongly recommend against this, or anything that leaves the resident with no incentive to vacate your property in good condition. Keep the security deposit intact, and return it to the resident in accordance with the lease terms.

If you calculate it out, the residents are only paying an additional two-month's rent to terminate the lease. Damages to the property should be treated as a separate issue when refunding the security deposit. Always keep them as separate talking points so your residents will not get confused.

Right to Inspection

There should be a clause in your lease that allows you the right to inspect the property with reasonable notice. The laws in some areas require very specific notice, such as at least 48 hours, prior to an inspection. In other areas, the inspection itself can only be conducted between certain times and days of the week. The common misconception among residents is that they are required to get 24-hours' notice for inspections or for any sort of entry. This might be good in practice, but it may not follow the law in your area.

So much misinformation is passed around the tenant community that this becomes a lesson in patience as much as anything based in law. If you don't believe me, post this as a question on Facebook in a "Houses for Rent" page and watch the diversity of answers. It's quite entertaining.

"Do I have to let my landlord in my house without notice?"

Answers will generally range from:

> "They MUST give 24-hours notice!" (not always true),

> to

> "Never! I don't have to allow them in if I don't want to!" (Hardly ever true).

Some tenants will say that such notice must be done by certified mail, and some that say their landlord can show up anytime they want. This misinformation is, however, not entirely their fault. Most of this is perpetuated because of landlords who don't know the law and are obtaining leases from outside their area. Contact your attorney, and have him answer the following items in particular, as some states are very specific:

- How much notice you are required to give your residents before entering?
- In what form does that notice need to be? Does it have to be in writing, or is a phone call acceptable?
- How does notice apply in emergency situations?
- Do you have to give an estimate as to how long you'll be there?
- Are you allowed to come and go, as in the case where you need to retrieve parts?
- What days of the week and times of day are you allowed to go to the property?
- What are the ramifications for not following the legally prescribed notification or entry procedures?

If your state laws are not specific, I recommend establishing a policy for what constitutes reasonable notice and the days and times you're able to enter the property. This is to prevent confusion when you visit the property, and what kind of notice your residents should expect.

Some areas require such notice to be in writing, which can be tricky if the resident really wants to be difficult and claim they didn't receive it. Some areas also require the notice to include the time and duration the landlord expects to be in the property.

As far as my research has led me, I have not found any areas where a resident can deny a landlord from entering and performing an inspection or maintenance if proper notice has been given. Of course, if a time is not convenient, the goal should not be to harass the tenant. Instead, a reasonable time should be worked out during business hours, say 8am to 6pm. You might not need to state the purpose of the inspection, although "Maintenance Inspection" seems to work quite well to get you the access you need.

Don't think that your inspections are going to yield some sort of "smoking gun" if you suspect the residents are doing something shady. This doesn't mean you shouldn't do the inspection, just don't expect to walk into a full-scale meth lab. You're there to look at the overall condition of the property and things that may be a cause for concern.

If you're there conducting a maintenance inspection, then make sure you're looking at maintenance-related items. Of course, it would be a cause of concern if you find there are more beds than would make sense for the number of people on the lease. The presence of a dog bowl or bag of cat food or a litter box when they aren't supposed to have any pets would be of similar concern. While these things might be clear lease violations, just be sure you are looking at things that are relevant and are based on how the property is being maintained.

It should go without saying that you should conduct yourself as a professional, even if the residents are not home. Rifling through their medicine cabinet or underwear drawer is not relevant and a great way to open yourself up to a lawsuit. No one wants to feel as though their trust has been violated, so stay on task and out of their personal things.

Managing Expectations

Chapter Twenty-Five
Bullet Points

Life is largely a matter of expectation.

- Horace, Roman Lyric Poet

The first three chapters of Part III are meant to focus you on several key areas where your lease needs to be in alignment with your business framework. This chapter is formatted to be more rapid-fire, giving you topics in a bullet-point approach for you to consider and discuss with your attorney when crafting or altering your lease.

- Right to Show Property - Similar to inspections, residents have certain rights regarding when landlords can show the property to prospective tenants. Some areas only require "reasonable notice" and others are much more specific. As stated in the Right to Inspection section, make sure you know the local laws, as there may be other limitations regarding marketing, advertising, and placement of signs for the property.
- Charges to Resident While in Possession - It is important to establish a clear policy in your lease about the payment of damages caused by the resident, whether the damages be physical or financial. For example, if the resident doesn't

mow the lawn and you get fined by the city because the grass is too high, that amount is then charged to the resident with the expectation that it gets paid immediately. Another example would include physical damages while they're still in possession of the property. Your attorney can help you work out the best way to word this in your lease.

- Use of the Premises – It is important to address the issue ensuring the property is being used exclusively as a private family residence and is not being used as a business. There is an array of legitimate home-based businesses out there which may be permissible, but the last thing you want is to have a daycare or retail operation being set up on your property without your knowledge or approval. Point out that the resident must comply with all the laws and ordinances of the appropriate governmental authorities affecting cleanliness, occupancy, and preservation. This could include things like mowing the lawn, removing trash cans from the street within a prescribed period of time, and the number of people living in a dwelling.

- Criminal Activity and Other Undesirable Behavior - Seriously consider addressing that immediate default of the lease will occur if criminal activity happens on the property by the resident, or their guests or visitors. Emphasize that eviction will follow such activity. I'd also recommend not allowing smoking inside the dwelling. If they do smoke inside, they will be charged for removing the smoke smell and any additional remediation, if necessary. Other things, such as going on the roof, might be something else to specifically prohibit.

- Number of Occupants - This can be difficult to enforce, especially for those people who will boldface lie to you about it and continue to deny it. The first thing you need to do is to define who is a temporary guest and who is an occupant. A standard I've used in the past is that a person is considered an occupant if they are receiving mail at that address. Another is if they are staying more than seven continuous days, or ten-days total within a 30-day period. Many residents will claim they have a "significant other" that has a place of their own, but they stay the night from time to time. Simply request they show proof such as a signed lease or utility bill that is in their name. Consider a penalty of $100 per unauthorized occupant per month to be enforced in these situations. This gives the lease some teeth so you don't have to file for eviction just to correct this situation.

- Attachment of Occupants - If you identify a Master Tenant in your lease, if your state allows such a lease, make sure that if the Master Tenant abandons the property or is otherwise inaccessible, the lease remains in force and shall attach to all the other adult occupants. Your attorney will be able to draft such language.

- Condition of Premises - One of the more aggravating parts of getting a property back from a resident is when they claim something was broken, damaged, or dirty when they moved in. This reason alone should compel you to realize that a move-in video is not just a good idea, it's essential. In addition to such a video, a move-in inspection checklist should be presented to the resident with an expectation of receiving it back within 72 hours of them taking possession. I suggest you require this to be sent via email to ensure that everyone has a copy and establishes a time-stamp. A sample move-in checklist is available for download at www.LandlordCoach.com/twiBook.

- Subletting - A sublease, or subletting, is a situation where your resident wants to leave and finds someone else to take over the lease. You can choose to allow subletting if you like, but I don't do it. I think it complicates matters unnecessarily as opposed to having people exercise the early termination option, as mentioned in the previous chapter. Plus, it eliminates the possibility of renting to someone that bypasses your screening and application process. Talk to your attorney about the legalities of this, but for all the risk, I don't see enough reward to allow subletting.

- Alterations and Improvements - I used to allow residents to paint, plant gardens, build shelves, and install patios. I quickly realized how terrible an idea this was when I found out how widely the quality of workmanship can vary. I had one family that insisted they paint their boys room blue, only to find out they painted everything blue – walls, ceiling, trim, doors, literally everything. Another resident did the same thing in black, except they painted the carpet and doorknobs too. In the lease, you may be able to require any alteration requests to be submitted in writing and that any requests must be approved in advance. You should also consider including verbiage allowing you the option to charge an additional amount for security in case such alterations are not returned to the original state when the resident moves. You could do the same thing with the installation of satellite dishes or cable wires.

- Dangerous Materials - One would think it to be common sense not to keep dynamite or anything explosive in your home, but sadly common sense isn't so common. Most times, this section serves as a reminder to residents not to keep gas cans stored in the home. For those homes without outdoor sheds, this might be the only choice that makes sense to keep their cans from being stolen or left out in the weather. Work up language with your attorney that makes sense for your particular property.

> Stop and Consider: I know some landlords try to restrict residents from having firearms on their rental property. I'm not going to get into a 2nd Amendment argument here, so I'll just say that I am against this restriction and move on. I don't feel that it's appropriate to restrict anyone that is lawfully in possession of a firearm, or limit their ability to defend themselves or their loved ones. If you do attempt to make such a restriction, keep in mind that there may be laws in your state prohibiting you from doing so.

- Damage to Premises - This section requires the resident to notify the landlord of any damage occurring to the property within a reasonable period of time, say within 12 hours. I try to limit using the word "reasonable" as much as possible when it's requiring the resident to perform some sort of action. To them, the fact that the roof has blown off might be reasonable not to report for 3 months. When you're putting this on the resident, I'd say 12 hours is reasonable.

- Pest Control - Rodents, ants, and other pests are a nuisance that may not be the fault of the resident. My Mom was obsessive about keeping a clean house. Plus, we always had at least a cat or two (or ten) living in and around the house when I was growing up. That said, we lived in the country, we still had the occasional mouse in our house.

Pest issues can get problematic if you leave it up to the resident to take care of on their own. Mice, for example, have a very short gestation period – around 20 days. When you consider that one single mouse averages a litter of about 7 mice, and that one female can have about 10 litters per year, suddenly you have a mouse population that has gotten completely out of hand.

Mice are just one example of pests that can get in a home. Stay in this business long enough and you'll experience everything from roaches to scabies to everyone's favorite pest, bed bugs. There are several ways to deal with such issues. Your solution just depends on your comfort level and understanding the risks involved in allowing residents to self-treat for insects or rodents. Here are some ideas that may work for you:

- o Give the resident 15 days from the date of initial possession to report any pests or rodents including: mice, ants, roaches, water bugs, fleas, bed bugs, and similar pests. Any costs of removal during that time shall be borne by the landlord. After that period, the costs shall be borne by the resident.

- o Wildlife such as birds, squirrels, bats, and raccoons shall be taken care of by the landlord. I don't recommend putting this on the resident since it's usually beyond their control and significant damage can result from ignoring this problem. If the resident thinks they are going to have to pay for it, they may conveniently ignore that such a problem exists.

- o Require the resident to report all insect problems and have a professional perform an inspection. Based on the professional's report you can then determine who should cover the cost of the remediation and removal.

- Holdover - Holdover is a situation where the Resident remains in possession of the unit after their original lease term has expired. This situation isn't unusual, and it seems that most states recognize that leases will default to a month-to-month tenancy. Month-to-month tenancy isn't necessarily a bad thing, but it does dull the purpose of having a lease to a certain extent.

It's important to understand that your lease is a contract; an agreement between you and your resident. It's legal documentation showing you're allowing someone to live in your property at a set price, for a predetermined period of time. Neither party, not you as the landlord, nor the resident, can unilaterally change those terms until the end of that predetermined time period.

With that frame of reference, it should seem obvious then for a landlord to always have the resident committed in a lease. However – whether it's due to ignorance or just poor organization – too many landlords allow their leases to expire. The expired lease, in most areas, then defaults to a month-to-month tenancy. The landlord, perhaps unaware of the change, gets no increase in rent for the added risk.

Think about it. Your tradeoff as a landlord is to keep the rent the same for one year, with your resident's commitment that they will live there for the entire time. Under a month-to-month tenancy, wouldn't it stand to reason you be compensated *more* for taking on the increased risk of allowing the resident to give you only 30 days-notice to vacate? Unfortunately, many landlords miss the boat by failing to get a premium for taking on this additional risk.

If you're a landlord and are experiencing a hot rental market then it may not matter much since the risk of having an extended vacancy is reduced, but there's no reason to leave money on the table if you don't have to. There's inherent value in allowing someone to live in your unit under a month-to-month tenancy versus being in a long-term lease, and the rent amount should be higher to reflect that value. I suggest an increase that makes it high enough to make the month-to-month tenancy workable for the resident, and enough to offset the risk if the resident moves outside of the prime leasing season. I have found a good rent premium for month-to-month tenancies to be ten percent of what you would normally rent a property for a one year lease. However, your rental market may allow for more.

- Surrender of Premises - It's a good idea to point out in your lease what constitutes surrender of the property back to you at the end of the lease term. For example, the residents should return all keys, provide a forwarding address, and perform a final inspection with the landlord. It's also not a bad idea, just to cover yourself, to have them sign a form indicating when possession was surrendered back to you. This helps establish a timeline for when the security deposit is to be returned to the resident.

- Abandonment - Abandonment can be a real pain because not only is the resident unresponsive to your phone calls, an inspection reveals they are halfway moved out of your property and it's not entirely clear if they are coming back. I suggest establishing several predetermined metrics that would reasonably define abandonment. An example might be if the resident is unresponsive for longer than 5 days, the property is lacking any one of the required utilities, **and** an inspection reveals an absence of furnishings that would reasonably suggest the property is occupied. Whatever you come up with, make sure it's enforceable uniformly across all your properties and residents.

- Smoke Detectors - There are some areas that require the installation of smoke detectors, but not all. Whether the law in your area requires it or not, installing them is just the right thing to do. In the absence of direction from local building codes, make sure you have at least one working smoke detector on each floor. Certain types of rental housing may also require providing carbon monoxide detectors as well as fire extinguishers. If you're not sure of the code, call the local city engineer, building inspector, or fire marshal and find out what they require in rental housing.

- Other - There will be a lot of other legal verbiage your attorney will put in the lease that you, nor I, nor anyone in non-barrister circles really understands. Clauses addressing severability, sole agreement, prevailing party, and modifications to the agreement – to name just a few – are as confusing as they are necessary. Discuss these with your attorney so you know what they represent should the need arise.

  Stop and Consider: There are times where a lease may need to be modified. In cases where a change request is initiated by the resident, I suggest charging an administrative fee for any modifications made to the lease during the lease term. Requests such as adding or removing people from the lease, adding or removing pets, changing the lease dates, or even getting copies of their lease can quickly get out of hand. It's amazing how once you start charging for things such as lease copies how quickly people find them on their own. You might consider emailing copies for free, but printing costs time and money. For the other types of requests, charging a fee keeps them to a minimum, and offsets the cost of what you're paying your VA to handle the administration and paperwork.

If you will have addenda to attach to your lease, such as Community Guidelines for the basic do's-and-don'ts or a Lead-Based Paint Disclosure, they could be referenced somewhere at the end of the lease. That way there's no disputing their presence, should the attachments come into question.

One last point: It's been said throughout this section many times, **hire an attorney** to do this for you so it's done correctly. There's no reason to throw away all your hard work simply because of a poorly worded lease agreement.

Managing Expectations

Chapter Twenty-Six

FAQs and SOP

**Rather than love, than money,
than fame, give me truth.**
- Henry David Thoreau

We've accomplished a great deal up to this point. First, we have developed a business framework that frees up much of your time. Second, you are on your way to developing a well-defined and purposeful lease, in which to communicate many of your expectations to your residents. The last piece is communicating expectations to your residents through your online FAQ (Frequently Asked Questions) listed on your website.

This is important is because there will be times when a policy or procedure is not on the lease but still needs to be communicated to your resident.

A good example would be:

"Why do you do a move-in or move-out video, and do I need to be present for it?"

or

"Why do you require me, or someone I know, to visit the property before I can submit an application?"

After reading this book, answers to these questions will now seem obvious to you, but will be foreign to your residents. The resident or applicant may see these policies as an unnecessary burden, even though you are simply trying to protect their interests.

Developing an Online FAQ

Developing an online FAQ has been mentioned in earlier chapters. The best way to start this is to work with your VA and have him chronicle his daily questions and your responses to them. To take this one step further, come up with a list of your own questions as a separate exercise. Get the juices flowing by writing down a few questions, and don't fill in the answers until later. Answering the questions will only slow down the process. Start writing and do not edit; aim for volume. You might be surprised by how many questions come to mind.

Here are some sample questions for your FAQ:

- Do all adult occupants need to be on the lease?
- Am I allowed to paint or do work on the property?
- Can I get another pet if I already have one? Will this increase my pet fees?
- If I get rid of my pet, will the monthly pet fee be removed?
- If I don't have a lawnmower, or don't have the time to cut the grass, can you recommend a lawn mowing service?
- How do I submit maintenance requests?
- Can I clean in lieu of paying the security deposit?

Answering the questions for your FAQ establishes policy, and each policy should be thought of in the context of your risk tolerance and business framework. Approaching your FAQ with this mindset will help keep all your policies in alignment with your infrastructure.

When you're writing in the answers for each of these questions, you're likely going to generate even more questions. Don't worry about trying to answer them, just get them down and answer them later. Stay focused on answering one question at a time to avoid becoming catatonic from task-overload. Once you come up with the answers, and have a fairly exhaustive list, leave the mental-hernia of categorizing them to your VA. This will help your VA become more familiar with your policies and your line of thinking. If you're having trouble coming up with answers to some of your questions, check out the resources page on www.LandlordCoach.com/twiBook.

> Stop and Consider: This is *not* just an exercise to give you something to do. Having a well-developed FAQ is one of the keys to getting your ticket punched to enter the realm of the Time-Wealthy. The more time you invest doing this up-front means the less time you'll have to spend answering the same questions, over and over, to your VA or your residents. This exercise is part of building the very foundation for your business. It will take time, like constructing a building, block by block, question by question. Yes, it's work, but I promise, it will be worth it.

Standard Operating Procedure (SOP)

Your Standard Operating Procedure (SOP) details how your business will run and covers things that might not be specifically stated on the lease or addressed in your FAQs. Your SOP will address policies that don't necessarily involve your residents, such as what to do with a rent check once it's been received from a resident, or how to pay a vendor after work has been completed at one of your properties. Your SOP will develop over time and should be added to, and modified by, you and your VA as things evolve. The modified SOP should then be saved with a new date as an entirely new document. This will provide a record of your amended procedures. Do NOT simply overwrite and save your SOP with no regard to the modification date. Any modifications done by your VA should first be approved by you.

Your SOP should cover everything from your company's mission statement, to your core values, to your HR policies. As you start looking at your business in a whole new light, you will think of things that need to be added to your SOP. Like you did with the FAQs, just write down the topic and don't worry about filling it all in until later. This is a process, so don't think you're going to be able to come up with a solid SOP in one sitting, one weekend, or even in one week. It's going to take time to develop; let it happen as situations come up or as you think about them. Carry a notepad, or keep one by your bed to jot down ideas as they come to mind. For a sample SOP that I developed over the years, please visit www.LandlordCoach.com/twiBook.

It's important to understand that your SOP is likely going to evolve significantly from where you start. There's nothing wrong with this; it's normal for your SOP to change as your business matures. Just like with a teenager, the things they once valued as a 10-year-old are no longer relevant as new things have now risen in importance. The same is true for your business as it develops and grows over time.

Your SOP – Begin with the End in Mind

Just like your FAQ, having a well-developed SOP pays huge time-dividends back to you. By having both well thought-out and firmly in place, specifically your SOP, it addresses many functional issues in the "Expectations" portion of the Process-Expectations-

Behavior paradigm. For a moment, let's go back and consider how it effects the Process.

Beginning with the end in mind, consider what you're trying to create for the reader of your SOP. Think about how your VA will be working from day to day and what that process will look like. If you're already established in the rental business then you'll know the types of calls your VA will be receiving. It's that line of thinking that will help you develop a meaningful and useful SOP. The Process section of this book contains many items that would logically go into your SOP. To engage the creative side of our brain, let's avoid reiteration and consider some other SOP items for a moment.

A good SOP item, for example, addresses your policy on allowing residents to clean in lieu of rent or payment of the security deposit. This is an issue that wouldn't be appropriate to address in your lease, and you might want to elaborate further on it as an item in your online FAQ. When you consider the answer to this and other policy-type questions that come up, remember that your reader isn't just your VA, it's also for the **future-you** which helps you stay consistent on your policies. Establish this in writing and save your brain-power for more important things.

Cleaning or Repairs in Lieu of Security Deposit/Rent

As an SOP item, for example, I strongly suggest you establish a formal policy to not allow residents to clean in lieu of paying the Security Deposit. I used to allow residents to do this and it seldom worked out in my favor. Even though I "paid" the resident for their labor by not collecting the security deposit, with very few exceptions, I got properties back in the same, unclean-state as when they first moved in, if not far worse. Without fail, the conversation went something like:

"Well, yeah the house is a mess but it's no worse than when we moved in!"

I believe the reason relates to the resident's perceived financial risk. Even though the agreement was for them to clean in lieu of the security deposit, they had no perceived financial risk to clean the property when they left because no money changed hands. Without any skin in the game, they would often ignore their responsibilities to clean when moving out since they felt they had nothing to lose.

I suggest if you're going to allow residents to clean, treat the cleaning and the move-in as two separate transactions. Have the residents pay what they owe in rent and security deposit, then, have them send you a detailed estimate for the cleaning *in advance*. Once they say the work is complete, inspect the property to ensure the work was done. Request an invoice detailing specifically what work they performed and compare it against the estimate they gave you to make sure they match up. Get them paid quickly and be sure to keep this invoice as proof that the property was cleaned should that ever come into question.

Similarly, I caution you to be wary of residents who offer you to "do work at the property" in lieu of payment of rent. Remember this phrase, it's one I got very comfortable saying to residents:

"Thanks for the offer, but unfortunately I can't buy bread with your labor..."

That usually shuts down the discussion pretty quickly.

Proration of Rent – Collection of First Month's Rent

Another example of an SOP item would be to address the payment of prorated rent. When residents are moving in on any day of the month other than the first, the resident should only be charged the prorated rent, which is fair. However, I made it a policy for the residents to pay the full month's rent up front, and pay the prorated rent in the second month of their tenancy. The reason for this is to prevent a resident from moving in near the end of the month, say the 26th, and only paying for 4 days of rent to get possession of a property. Consider the following example:

Let's say our new resident is moving in on June 12th, and the rent is $3,400. The resident would pay $3,400 up front, plus any required Security Deposit and last month's rent, if applicable, and they would only pay $2,040 on the first of the following month. After that, the rent would return as normal. See the below diagram for more clarification.

June 12th – Move-in	$3,400 Rent Paid
July 1st	$2,040 Prorated Rent Paid
August 1st	$3,400 Rent Paid

Hiring, Vetting, and Paying Subcontractors

In the Process section of the book, we discussed how working with maintenance vendors can be a challenge, especially if you're used to doing all the work yourself. The SOP should address the screening process for your vendors using the Maintenance Survey, collecting their insurance and tax information, and verifying the work has be performed.

The process in your SOP might look something like this:

-   Maintenance request is received at the office.
-   Maintenance request is entered into PM Software, generating a Work Order.

- Work Order is assigned to a maintenance vendor.
- Work Order is sent to maintenance vendor via email with instructions that vendor contacts resident directly to schedule the work. The vendor is to contact the office both when the work is scheduled and when the work is complete.
- For large tasks or repairs over $350, an estimate should be prepared and approved by the manager.
- For non-emergency tasks, the maintenance vendor should complete the task within 72 hours. For emergency tasks, it should be addressed within 24 hours. Follow up should be scheduled with the vendor as appropriate.
- When the vendor reports the work is complete, contact the resident immediately to ensure the repair is done.
- Match up invoice to estimate, if applicable. Schedule payment within 7 days of receipt.
- Ensure vendor's insurance information is up-to-date before issuing payment.
- Issue the payment to the vendor.

This process can be added to or adjusted as necessary to fit your situation, but be wary of vendors that attempt to bypass your policies. I recognize there are worthwhile vendors who still prefer to do business on a handshake, or only want to deal with you and not your VA. Keep in mind that we're trying to build a scalable business here – one that runs without your constant input and management. If you're used to working with a particular vendor that runs fast-and-loose and only wants to hear from you, you should consider the real cost of doing business with this individual. Perhaps they are good at fixing things, but horrible at giving detailed-billing or contacting the office. Whatever their shortcomings, just remember, the more you have to manage someone, the less valuable they are to your business.

This concludes the section on Expectations in our PEB model. There may be other ways outside of your FAQ and SOP that you choose to communicate your expectations to your residents, vendors, or anyone you work with, but always keep it simple. The degree of clarity with which you communicate your expectations directly relates to how effective you are as a boss. The next section of this book goes to the heart of the last portion of the PEB model: Behavior.

Part IV – Behavior

Chapter Twenty-Seven

Managing Your Emotions

Behavior is what a man does, not what he thinks, feels, or believes.

- Emily Dickinson

Standing at the door of his office, Jack stood, his broad smile marking a milestone he reached today. A milestone worthy of celebration. Just six months ago his life was a mess. It was a period defined by being run by his real estate business and constantly at the beck and call of his residents.

Today however, is a different story, thus the celebration. It's 5:30 on Saturday morning and Jack is prepared to go to the driving range with his brother-in-law. Moving from the door, he now stands at the desk in his home office. He looks over a small stack of opened, neatly-piled mail, the word "SENT" stamped in bold red ink across the top of each letter. His smile relaxes to a look of satisfaction, knowing that each one of these letters has been scanned and is now sitting in the email inbox of his VA for her to handle.

It was only six months ago when Jack made the decision to invest in the infrastructure that fundamentally changed the way he operated his business. He thinks back to a time when he was afraid to even open the mail. Now, he's comforted with the knowledge that one of his few critical tasks is to open and scan incoming mail, sending anything his VA can handle directly to her via email. Sarah, his VA, is now handling 90% of the correspondence that crosses Jack's desk.

Leaving the office, Jack turns off the light and closes the door. Anything that is an emergency has been handled or is in the process of being handled. It's taken a little bit of tweaking and trial and error, but Jack is approaching an almost Zen-like state. He is starting to see the benefits of being a Time-Wealthy Investor.

The one thing he wished he could control is the emotional roller coaster he occasionally experiences when he has to speak to one of his residents. Jack realized that the emotional connection he has with his residents is a double-edged sword. He has become so familiar with them he knows nearly everything about them – and they know much about him. Getting that genie back in the bottle was going to be a tough thing to do.

He that will not command his thoughts will soon lose the command of his actions.

- Thomas Wilson

Influencing Behavior

This might be the most difficult part of the PEB Model, simply because of the emotional component involved. As frustrating as it can be, you must stay in control of your emotions if you are going to get the desired behavior you're seeking from your residents. Trust me; I get it. You spent an entire week piecing back together the property a previous resident destroyed, only to get a resident that curses you out on the phone and refuses to pay rent. As much as you may want to, you need to resist the temptation to drive over to your property and staple an eviction notice to your tenant's hand.

It can be a lesson in frustration to attempt to control someone else's behavior if you're not in control of your own; just ask any parent of a teenager. Trying to control someone else's behavior can be like pushing a rope. In any given situation, you really only have control over your own behavior. By controlling your own behavior, however, you can influence that of others.

Being in control of your emotions to influence others isn't a profound thought – far from it. If you have an interaction with someone, and your behavior is irrational or out of control, you can't expect them and the people around you to not be impacted by that. I'm not saying that, by default, they will be irrational or out of control, but you shouldn't be surprised if they mimic some of the behavior you're exhibiting. The point here is that you can't possibility hope to get the behavior you want out of someone else if your own behavior is less than desirable.

Wise men speak because they have something to say. Fools because they have to say something.

- Plato

The Communication Pie

In the early 1960's, Professor Albert Mehrabian was conducting research at UCLA on the subject of non-verbal communication. He is best known for his work developing what became known as "the communication pie." His study was conducted to find out how much non-verbal communication mattered in conversations where someone was conveying what they think or how they feel about a given topic.

His findings turned the world upside-down. In the context of a conversation about feelings or attitudes, only 7% of the message was communicated through spoken words. Only 7%! His point was not to diminish the impact of the words we use, but to point out the importance of **how** we say our words, and ensuring our body language is in alignment with how we are saying them.

Here's the summary of his study:

- 7% of a message pertaining to feelings and attitudes is in the words that are spoken
- 38% of a message pertaining to feelings and attitudes is paralinguistic (the way words are said)
- 55% of a message pertaining to feelings and attitudes is in facial expression

While communicating with your residents, influencing behavior is more about **how** you speak and behave than specifically **what** you say. In the context of your VA, if they will be speaking a great deal with your residents, be sure you're selecting one who has excellent customer service skills.   Also, their ability to communicate on the phone must be solid and easily understood by your residents.   The last thing you want is to have a misunderstanding because of something that was said by your VA.

The Collections Agent

Back in 2009, when my whole world was going to crap, I owed money to seemingly everybody. I half-joked at the time that it would have been easier to get everyone I **didn't** owe money to into a room rather than all the people I did owe. I was in various stages of foreclosure on multiple properties. Credit card companies, banks, and all sorts of creditors were beating down my door for their money. Every day was a new call, which I would send to voicemail, then ignore it. I simply didn't have the money to pay anyone. It was horrible.

One day, there was a glimmer of hope. I somehow ended up with enough money one month to pay BOTH my electric and my water bill, with a little money left over. I'd been broke for so long I wasn't sure how to act. I knew it was time to start taking my creditors' calls and begin getting them squared up.

I owed an ungodly amount of money. Between all the credit cards and deficiency judgements from foreclosures, the number was in the millions. I had decided early on that bankruptcy was not going to be an option I would entertain. Given that, this was going to be no easy task. I resolved to take the next phone call from a creditor, no matter who it was.

The very next morning, a few minutes after 8 o'clock, the phone rang. Not recognizing the number, I took the call.

"Hello Mr. Dolfini?" the friendly voice asked politely.

"Yes, this is Mark." I replied

She continued, "Hello sir, my name is Patricia and I'm calling from the 'blah blah' Law Office. Did I catch you at a bad time?"

I was taken aback. She was asking if she caught me at a bad time. None of the other collections people ever did that.

"Um, no." Searching for the right words, "Thanks for asking. Now is fine."

She continued, "Well that's great sir. Like I said, my name is Patricia and I do apologize, but I need to tell you really quick that this is an attempt to collect a debt, and any information we gather would be used for that purpose. So now that we're all legal, obviously I wanted to talk to briefly about your account. Do you have a few minutes to go over that with me? I promise, it won't take long at all."

What the living hell is going on? I thought to myself. She's asking permission to talk to me? Regaining my composure,

"Um, sure, yeah I've got a few minutes. What account is this?"

"Well that's great," Patricia said, "Yes, this is for the 'X' credit card account. I really appreciate you taking the time to talk with me about this. I know talking about money isn't always an easy conversation to have, but I promise we will go over a few things and then you can be on your way is that okay?" Once again asking permission.

"Sure..." I replied cautiously.

We spent the next few minutes verifying my account and contact information, and she was so incredibly polite I wondered if this poor woman lost a bet. Perhaps doing community service for some sort of grotesque crime. I could hear her typing as she updated my contact information, and keeping me updated as to how much longer the call would go.

After a few minutes, she took a deep breath and sighed.

"So," she started slowly, "I know you realize that we need to somehow figure out how to get this balance worked out. And I'm just going to ask the question, but is there *any* way at all you can pay this account in full today?" She was a master, struggling with words I knew she said a least a thousand times, but she did it so she didn't sound scripted.

The balance due was several thousand dollars, I had a little bit of money, maybe $200 or so, but nothing close to the payoff.

"No," I answered, "I'm afraid not. I just don't have that sort of money right now."

"Hmmm… I understand," she let out, sounding a little disappointed, "things are a tough out there right now." She continued, "Here's the thing; my manager has a list of accounts, and he just wanted to send this straight to the lawyers and get a judgment." She paused, "I'm not going to insult you; they know you owe the money. Heck, *you* know you owe the money. There's no sense in getting a judge to agree to that fact, it's just going to get a lot more expensive for you, plus you'd have to go to court and all that."

She continued, again, struggling to get the words out.

"I told him that if I could just talk to you, maybe we could work something out. Is there something I could go back to him with, any amount at all, that you could pay today? I'd love to see you get something paid toward this balance and have us off your back. I know how good that would feel for you."

Boy was she right, that *would* feel good! Amazing in fact. It was a great feeling as well, to think someone on the inside was rooting for me. Patricia was a master at communicating effectively. Not in a manipulative way, but in a way that would get the behavior from me that was most needed.

What Patricia clearly understood is the behavior she needed to bring, in order to get the behavior from me that she wanted. She wanted me to pay this off, not just for her and her law firm, but for *me*. She understood that by coming to me with the right mix of positive attitude, behavior, and technique, my account was likely one of dozens that she would resolve that day alone.

By the time we hung up from that very first phone call, I had made a $100 payment toward my $2,000 debt. She assured me that it would be credited right away, ensured that I had her direct phone number, and that we could revisit this conversation in a few weeks. She asked a good time of day when she could call back, and that she would try very hard to keep within a certain window. Patricia was not only exceedingly polite and friendly, she was impressive as a professional, and no doubt spectacularly effective.

By the end of that year I had gotten that account paid off before any others. I almost looked forward to my bi-weekly call from Patricia. We'd laugh and talk about this and that. She would tell me how proud of me she was that this account was getting paid off, $100 here, $250 there. She always asked if there was any way I could pay the account in full so they could report it paid in full. My answer was always no, but instead of her sounding disappointed, it was *me* that sounded disappointed. She had gotten the behavior from me that she needed, and it worked out amazingly for both of us.

The Success Triangle: ABT – Attitude Behavior Technique

Long after my account with Patricia was stamped Paid-in-Full, I took a sales training class to learn the Sandler Sales method. If you're not familiar with David Sandler, he is brilliant at solutions-based selling, although it goes much deeper than that. Whether or not you're in a professional sales role I highly recommend you take this training if it's offered near you. It will not only help with your real estate business, but with life in general.

One thing I learned from Sandler is the "Success Triangle," with each of the three points being Attitude, Behavior, and Technique. The idea is that to be successful in your interactions, whether it be sales, collections, or negotiations, each of these three points must be present.

It should be obvious from my interactions with Patricia that she possessed all three of these things in her conversations with me. Her attitude was great – positive and upbeat. Her behavior reflected that attitude, and although we became more casual as time went on, she always maintained an air of professionalism. Both of these things, combined with keen negotiating skills (technique), made her fiercely effective when it came to collecting on past due accounts.

The ABT Triangle is Excerpted from the Sandler training program, President's Club Professional Development Program, Trainer's Guide, © 2000, Sandler Systems, Inc. All rights reserved.

On my last payment to Patricia (I had long-forgotten that I was actually paying a law firm) I asked her, "Of all the jobs you could be doing, why are you doing this? I mean, this profession sounds like it sucks, but you have such a wonderful attitude!"

"Aww," she said genuinely, "you're so nice to say that. Honestly though, I love what I do. I feel I'm helping people during what is obviously a very rough time for them."

Pausing for a moment, she continued. "As for my attitude, I just choose to be happy. Some people may try to do this job using a different approach, but that would just put me in a bad mood. I don't always get it back from the people I call on but I don't take it personally. I could be the fifth person they heard from that day wanting money. The last thing I want to do is make them feel bad." She chuckled to make her point.

I nodded as she spoke, I knew everything she was saying was authentic. She was a profound person; one I was very glad to have met.

> **There is an immutable conflict at work in life and in business, a constant battle between peace and chaos. Neither can be mastered, but both can be influenced. How you go about that is the key to success.**
>
> **- Phil Knight, Co-Founder and former CEO of Nike, Inc.**

Mimic the Behavior You Want

Patricia treated me with respect, so she got it in return. Patricia never swore at me, or got frustrated, so I never did either. It was an odd relationship, if you want to call it that, but a very valuable one. I doubt she realized it, but she taught me a great deal during our interactions.

With Patricia, I thought at first her effectiveness was simply based on how she said something versus what she actually said. Then I realized it went much deeper than that. She chose an attitude that served her and those around her quite well. In the world of collections, you can only fake it for so long. I feel it's the same in the rental business.

All of this relates to your real estate business in many profound ways. Always consider what emotions you may be causing in others with your attitude, behavior, and technique. Furthermore, always give people the ability to retain their dignity. There's no point in beating someone down to the point where they have nothing left inside. I will forever remember the way Patricia treated me. She always left me with my dignity – something I suspect she did with everyone she spoke to.

The underlying point of all of this is to be self-aware. To influence someone's behavior, your own behavior must align with the behavior you're wanting in return. Don't let the world around you dictate your attitude. Mastery at anything requires first the ability to control your emotions. Make a conscious decision to choose the attitude you want, and you'll be much happier and fulfilled – not only in business, but in life.

Behavior

Chapter Twenty-Eight

The Art of Negotiation

If there is any one secret to success, it lies in the ability to get the other person's point of view and see things from that person's angle as well as from your own.

- Henry Ford

There are volumes of books written about negotiation that I won't even attempt to replicate. There are some basics about negotiation, however, that will help you get closer to your vision for the future.

First of all, not every encounter with your resident needs to be a formal negotiation. Sometimes just having a simple conversation will accomplish all that you and your residents need. If you treat every single interaction with your residents as if it's going to be a Federal Court case, you're not going to serve your residents, or your vision for that matter, very well at all. Resurrect the lost art of conversation, especially the listening part. You might be surprised how well it works when interacting with your residents.

A person or organization that approaches conflicts with a win-win attitude possesses three vital character traits:

1. **Integrity: sticking with your true feelings, values, and commitments**
2. **Maturity: expressing your ideas and feelings with courage and consideration for the ideas and feelings of others**
3. **Abundance Mentality: believing there is plenty for everyone**

> - Steven Covey, Habit #4, *The 7 Habits of Highly Effective People*

Prepare for Win-Win

I can't say it much better than Steven Covey, but when it comes to negotiating, nothing will happen if either side is feeling like they're being left behind. This is where you consider the context of win-win in your negotiations. Having integrity, maturity, and an abundance mentality will serve you well in negotiations. Having empathy, however – considering the other side of the argument – is the critical component to making sure everyone gets what they need in the discussion, and no one feels left out. This tees up your negotiations for a win-win mindset.

Before having an important conversation with your resident, make sure you know your desired outcome beforehand. Think big picture. What is it you're really trying to accomplish? This is where having a sound sense of your "Why" comes into play. Use your vision for the future as a guide if things start to get hazy during the negotiation.

Long before you walk into a room to start negotiating with someone, you should have a clear idea of three possible outcomes; the ideal outcome, an outcome you could live with, and an outcome that is the base minimum for you. If you start a discussion without having clarity about what you want, clarity in the discussion is not going to magically appear from the ether. Not a good approach.

Recognize early on that it's your fault if anyone in the room, either you or your resident, is feeling as though they're getting screwed with their pants on. The pressure of the situation may be something that you haven't considered until you're well into the conversation. This is why you need to decide what you want in advance, and avoid winging it. Being prepared prior to the meeting will help keep your emotions in check and your negotiations around a win-win context.

We don't point a pistol at our own forehead. That is not the way to conduct negotiations.

- Benjamin Netanyahu

Don't Negotiate Against Yourself

Don't assume you know what your residents want. This is a critical mistake and one you need to avoid. Too many times I've given away the store when it wasn't necessary. Consider the following story:

The resident calls to inform you that their sewer is backed up for the fourth time that week. You've done your best to make the situation right, but the next available plumber is still another three days out from showing up. The resident calls a meeting over at their house because of the ordeal, and you're sure you're about to get your ass verbally handed to you.

You walk in, sit down, and before anyone utters a word, you immediately offer to put them up in a hotel for the next three nights. After all, you're sure this is where the conversation is going. They are very pleased with your generosity and quickly take you up on it. Come to find out, they really only wanted to be compensated $25 for having to do their laundry at the laundromat.

Don't assume you know what your residents want.

People aren't always unreasonable, so don't jump to the conclusion that they want to exact a pound of flesh from you. Sometimes all it would take is to ask, "How can I make this right?" Let their answer guide you in terms of where to take the negotiation. Many times – in fact, most times – people don't really know what they want because **they** haven't thought about what **they** want. In reality, asking that question often catches them off guard. Give them a few minutes to consider it. If they can't come up with an answer, start the negotiation with the best of your three possible outcomes and work from there.

Although we're talking about people's houses and state of living, while important, we're not talking about life and death here. Most decisions about properties don't need to be made in haste or in short-order. Let's say you thought out, in advance, your three possible outcomes, but the resident comes to you with an offer you hadn't considered. If you need some time to consider what your residents want, just say so. Let them know you need time, perhaps a day or so, to consider what they're asking and tell them you hadn't considered their offer as an option. If you're getting pressure from them to make a decision, state that you need to consult your business partner or accountant before making any sort of decisions relating to the lease or making concessions.

If, however, the situation warrants making a timely decision, step outside the room and make a phone call, walk around the block, or take a short drive. Most times just removing yourself from the scene can bring clarity you won't get by standing in front of your resident. Don't be ridiculous about this, though. If what your resident wants is reasonable, and is within your predetermined high and low water marks for your outcome, just agree to it and move on.

Negotiate from a Position of Strength

You want to negotiate from a position of strength whenever you can. Sometimes, however, that's just not possible. For example, let's say you had to evict someone in the middle of January. You have a vacancy to fill during a bad time of the year, and are looking at a potentially empty unit for the next three months. You might just be willing to take $800 for the first three months on a rental that normally rents for $1,200. Or you are willing to take a short-term lease for $1,300 per month, but you pay all the utilities. Negotiating from strength can take many forms, from holding negotiations in your office or a place that you control, to the time of year, or even time of day. Do the best you can to control all the factors that help you negotiate from strength to tip the balance in your favor.

Keep in mind what outcome you're wanting to accomplish. Meeting at their home, although perceptively a weak position, is actually a position of strength if you're wanting to show your sincerity. This could be important when you need to avoid the appearance of being authoritative, such as when you're trying to atone for making a large mistake. Again, having an idea of what you're wanting to accomplish beforehand will keep the meeting focused and on track. If things start to go sideways in the conversation, simply address it and move the meeting to another time or venue. Simply state, "I'm sorry, I'm not in the right frame of mind to have this discussion right now. Something in my day has me preoccupied and I'm afraid I'm going to need to reschedule."

Although it's important to negotiate from strength, that doesn't mean from a position of absolute dominance. If you are controlling the location, time and date, and all the items in the lease, don't pull a Scrooge and steal their last lump of coal. If your meeting is really more about you just trying to show off your power, then your customers are likely to resent you and eventually go elsewhere. Don't ever paint someone into a corner. Like my collections-agent friend Patricia, always leave them with their dignity.

> **Just a reminder, what other people think of you is none of your business.**
>
> **- Ze Frank, American Humorist**

Need for Acceptance

You can't possibly hope to negotiate anything to your benefit if your need for acceptance exceeds your ability to negotiate toward your vision. We all want to be treated fairly, but if you are afraid to negotiate a deal because you're afraid that your residents won't like you, you're likely to get steamrolled every single time.

This is where a lot of investors fail and become increasingly frustrated. One of the biggest things keeping us from holding people accountable is our need for acceptance from others. If you're trying to enforce late fees and your need for acceptance is higher than your need to collect, guess what happens? That's right; you'd better get used to late rent payments.

Treating your rules very matter-of-factly and letting the system work the way it's supposed to helps you bypass the need for acceptance. These people are your customers, not your friends or family. You don't owe them anything but a solid, consistent process and a good product. If you have failed to deliver on either of those, then yes, perhaps concessions make sense until you get those things in order.

On the other end of the spectrum, there are people with very little need for acceptance, which can be equally problematic. Remember that the real estate business is a people-business, requiring good and consistent customer service. If you are the type of person who leaves a trail of destruction whenever you leave a room, I suggest you leave the negotiating to your VA or someone you trust. It's okay to be firm, but no one wants to deal with a jerk.

Behavior

Chapter Twenty-Nine

Avoiding Drama

Never argue with a fool; onlookers may not be able to tell the difference.

- Mark Twain

Drama is the one thing I will go to great lengths to avoid. Not only is it unproductive, it is exhausting. Some people can become quite addicted to drama, and if you know someone like that, I suggest you do your best to avoid them. If that's not possible, as would be the case of your residents, there is a way to deal with the drama-seeker. First, let's understand how drama is created.

The Drama Triangle

In order for drama to exist, three things must be present. There must be a Victim, an Antagonist, and a Hero. If any one of these components is missing, drama cannot exist.

The first of the three components is the Victim. A Victim, in this context, is a person who's had something happen to them. It doesn't matter what that "something" is, and it doesn't need to be particularly horrible. It only needs to be **perceived** to be horrible by the Victim. Keep in mind what a Victim perceives to be egregious, you might find to be quite benign. In fact, your lack of sympathy could cause the Victim to become even further victimized, and so the cycle perpetuates.

The Antagonist in this context is the person, thing, or situation that is persecuting the Victim. It could be anything really, so try not to think of an Antagonist only as a bully stealing lunch money. It is the *Victim*, no one else, who defines who the Antagonist is and what he is doing, which is causing him to be victimized.

The final piece of the drama triangle is the Hero. This is the person that "saves" the Victim from the Antagonist. The Hero sympathizes with the Victim, taking on their pain as if it were their own. Like any good rescuer, the Hero rides in on their white horse, defeating the Antagonist and saving the Victim, riding off into the sunset like any good Western movie.

Now that we have our players defined, the drama triangle works like this. The Victim, let's call him Vince gets verbally accosted by the Antagonist, Alan. It doesn't matter what happened, but let's say that Alan called Vince "stupid". Vince, completely offended, goes to seek out a Hero.

In steps Herald, our Hero. Vince goes to Herald, telling him how offended he is that Alan called him "stupid." Herald, offended himself, takes on Vince's pain and anguish, and now goes straight to Alan to confront him. Now, the drama starts.

I'll spare you the back and forth between Alan, Herald and Vince as I'm sure you can fill in the blanks. Usually it would be some variation of Alan denying he said that to Vince, and Herald trying to set things straight. This becomes a circus as Vince and Alan argue, using Herald, the Hero, as the medium. Welcome to the Drama Triangle; enjoy your stay.

Before you try to set things straight, be sure you see things straight.

- Unknown

Avoiding the Drama Triangle

I'm not sure where I learned that last quote, but it has saved me countless times from being sucked into someone else's drama. In addition, know that drama cannot exist if any one of the three components is missing. While you can't control the Victim or the Antagonist, you **can** have direct control over the Hero. That is, if the Hero is you. If someone else wants to be the Hero, as far as I'm concerned, let them, especially if it keeps you out of it.

Empathy not Sympathy

I was having lunch with a good friend of mine who runs two restaurants very close to Purdue University. We got on the subject of people bringing nonsense to our doorsteps, and we started talking about the Drama Triangle. She made me aware of another phrase with which I want you to become comfortable. Feel free to paraphrase to suit your own manner of speaking. When someone brings a problem of theirs to you, after you are done listening, and when it's appropriate, respond with one of the following:

> "Wow, I understand why you'd be upset. How do you intend to work through this?"

> "Oh boy, I could see why you'd think that is terrible. I'm very sorry this has happened. I understand that this isn't your fault, how do you plan to get this figured out?"

> "Wow, I am very sorry to hear about that. I can certainly understand why you'd be upset. I know this

> isn't your fault or even something that is under your
> control, what are you doing to come up with a
> solution?"

All of these responses are polite, friendly, empathetic, and most importantly, it keeps you out of it! This puts the problem squarely back onto the would-be Victim. It also forces them to get specific about what they are wanting from you. If their answer involves me handling their problems for them, I might offer suggestions, but I will continue to put the issue back on them.

If, for example, the Victim talks about their car being broken down, this does not mean you can't empathize, but it doesn't mean you take on their responsibility as a car owner.

> "Oh, your car broke down? Oh, I hate when that
> happens. What are you doing to work through that?"

Notice that **I'm not offering to solve anything for them**. I simply empathize and ask them what they plan to do to fix it. This does NOT define me as the Hero. There is a subtle, but important, difference in asking them how they plan to solve it, versus helping them by interjecting myself in an area I have no business being involved in.

Using your stock phrase to redirect the problem doesn't mean you lack compassion for your resident. You can be helpful by getting your VA to research a bus route for them, or finding a towing service to get their car to a reputable mechanic. There are many ways you can be helpful that cost you a minimum amount of time and money, and keeps you out of the Drama

Triangle. Offer suggestions, but do NOT take on their problems as your own.

> Stop and Consider: Serial-Victims aren't interested in solving the problems they have as much as they want the emotional payoff that comes with being a Victim. The payoff of having a Hero inject themselves into the situation creates the drama they are seeking, whether it's a conscious thought or not.

> If you're dealing with a resident that is a Serial-Victim, you really must be careful. Victims, in this context, don't want to be held accountable to their problems. By holding a Victim accountable, or putting the problem back on them, you might unwittingly become the Antagonist in their eyes. The Victim then seeks out another Hero, which is great except this time *you* become the cause of the drama. For the Serial-Victim, it's an endless loop and one you want to avoid.

Bad things happen all the time. The best tool to keeping you out of the Drama Triangle is understanding the difference between sympathy and empathy. Sympathy is pity or feeling sorry for another person. Empathy is simply emotionally relating to someone. Consider how your need for acceptance may come into play here. If you have a high need for acceptance from your residents, you are much more likely to get drawn into the Drama Triangle because you want them to like you. It's easy to get your residents to like you if you're solving their problems for them. You can be helpful, but let them help themselves. Be vigilant, and stay out!

> **Most people do not listen with the intent to understand; they listen with the intent to reply.**
>
> **- Steven R. Covey**

The Lost Art of Listening

Something to keep in mind when dealing with people, is that you need to develop good listening skills. The hospitality industry teaches this to their new recruits from day one. So many times, especially in today's fast-paced, technology-driven world, people just want to be heard. I "borrowed" the LEARN process from the hospitality industry, but modified to fit my specific needs. When handling a customer's issue I refer to LEARN:

L – Listen – Actively listening, not interrupting, making sure they have a chance to tell the entire story. In the words of Steven Covey, "Seek first to understand, then to be understood."

E- Empathize, not Sympathize – Saying "I can understand why you'd be upset," or "Oh my, how frustrating!"

A – Apologize – A simple "I'm so sorry for the error," or "My sincere apologies for the issue."

R – Restate – Restate the problem to the customer in your own words so they know that you understand their problem.

N – Notify – Who needs to know about this? Inform your maintenance person, the authorities, or whoever should know.

I taught this process to my maintenance technicians and office staff to enhance their listening skills when working with residents, owners, and vendors. It's amazing how many potential problems are diffused when you simply talk less – and listen more. The LEARN process is an easy mechanism to use when you're dealing with an upset resident.

Silence is one of the great arts of conversation.

– Marcus Tullius Cicero

Although the LEARN process is a simple and effective tool, there are times where you find yourself dealing with a resident who is argumentative to the point of being combative. As difficult as this is, you must resist the urge to get drawn into this sort of behavior and respond in kind.

Of course, we're human. It's natural for us to retaliate or at least defend ourselves when a resident screams at us, but you can't let this sort of nonsense get to you. Just listen quietly – go back to your vision – remember that engaging with them in this manner has no place in where you see yourself in the future. Know that if you maintain your professionalism in the conversation, you have an emotional place for the resident to come back to after they have calmed down. If you both unleash hate on each other, they've seen that you can be manipulated. You've both seen each other at your worst, and in a business relationship there's seldom an ability to recover from that.

If things deteriorate to the point where you or your VA has been threatened with physical harm, call the police and let them handle it. If you are recording your calls, you can share those with the authorities. In the case where they are not threatening but are swearing and using inappropriate language, simply let them run their course and remind them that you're not swearing at them. Stay calm, empathize with them, but you don't need to be anyone's whipping boy. If they can't bring the conversation to a professional level, simply hang up. Let them call back when they've had time to cool off. I think the following quote from Moliere is a great way to sum up this section of the book:

A wise man is superior to any insults which can be put upon him, and the best reply to unseemly behavior is patience and moderation.

- Moliere, French Actor and Playwright. Considered the greatest of all writers of French Comedy.

Chapter Thirty

The Last Chapter

Perfection is not attainable, but if we chase perfection we can catch excellence.

- Vince Lombardi

Captain Jack

Jack is well on his way to the Promised Land of paid-in-full rental properties. His real estate business runs like a well-oiled machine. He feels more like a mechanic that tinkers with things from time to time when problems come up that his system should have otherwise caught. He still has an issue here and there, but nothing like his days of drama of the past. His residents are happier, his relationships with his coworkers are better, and he is much more intentional in his marriage. Now that Jack understands what it means to be Time-Wealthy, he has stopped putting off all the things he wanted "someday". Now that he has time to do the things he enjoys about his business, like finding rental properties and making deals, he is already implementing his expansion plans. The most exciting news however, is that Jack and his wife have expansion plans of their own – Jack and his wife are now expecting their first child.

Jack has come to understand that a pile of money and excessive cash flow are largely meaningless if you have no time to spend it, or are spending it on materialistic nonsense that brings only fleeting moments of happiness. True wealth is Time-Wealth. The ability to control your calendar and to do what you want, when you want, and with whom you want is the real pot of gold worth seeking. This is what Jack has finally realized, and he has never looked back.

Someday Jack will likely leave his day job, but he's got time to plan for that. He likes what he does at work, but he really enjoys the lifestyle that his real estate business now offers him.

Chasing Perfection

Your business will never be perfect. There will always be things in your system which you will, at some point, need to tweak, adjust, or simply remove. This requires vigilance on your part to periodically reexamine the way you're doing things. I can think of one glaring example where this manifested itself in my own business.

For years, I had mail sent to a post office box. One day, my Operations Manager mentioned she was overwhelmed at the office and asked if I wouldn't mind getting the mail for her. I didn't have a lot going on at that particular moment, so I agreed.

All our correspondence went to our post office box: bills, rent checks, legal notices, paychecks from our outsourced payroll provider, literally everything. Unless it was hand-delivered to our office by a vendor, a resident, or junk mail from the mailman, it came through the post office box.

After retrieving the mail, on my way back from the post office to the office, it occurred to me that this was something that she did every single day. The post office wasn't far from our building, maybe a ten minute-drive. Add parking and walking to the post office, another five minutes. If I had to get in line to buy stamps or sign for the occasional certified package, add another ten minutes on top of that. Add back the 15 minutes or so to walk back to the car and drive time back to the office, and I calculated an average of 45 minutes PER DAY being wasted simply because our mail was not being delivered to our office. The cost of the box was immaterial, maybe $60 per year, but the *real* cost was the lost time from having to go there every day.

Our post office box cost $8,820 per year in lost productivity when I considered the opportunity cost for my Operations Manager leaving the office to go get the mail. What a monumental waste! I immediately directed my staff to send out notices to anyone sending mail to the post office box to cease and desist, and instead, send any and all correspondence directly to our office.

Thinking back, I secured the post office box five years previous as one of my initial pieces of infrastructure to avoid having people show up at my house. Though I'd since moved to an office, it simply never occurred to me to stop using my post office box.

Obsolescence is something to be constantly aware of when maintaining a system. Don't lose track of what you're doing and why you're doing it. Chances are, when you consider all the activities you're doing, many can be streamlined or eliminated altogether. After a period of growth, be intentional and act like a 3-year old, asking "why?" about everything you're doing. This isn't for just your real estate business either, consider applying this to your work and home life as well. If you get a lot of answers starting with "Well, it's the way we've always done it..." chances are you have some room to improve or eliminate that given task entirely.

Wealth is the ability to fully experience life.

- Henry David Thoreau

Parting Thoughts

We have covered a good deal of ground since the start of our journey, and there is much to consider in your quest for Time-Wealth. I hope you have found the tools and ideas in this book useful. Keep things simple and resist getting hung up on the details that cause stagnation. Start with your vision for the future, and go back to it when you're feeling stuck. Not everything you put in place will be perfect at the start. Don't let the fear of failure prevent you from moving and improving.

I encourage you to go back through this book and do not be afraid to highlight, make notes, and draw pictures that will help you retain what you've learned. Make this book your own, then plan to put it down and go into the real world. Come back to it when you need to, just like you would a map. If you ever need more support, I'm just a few clicks away. Just go to www.LandlordCoach.com/twiBook for more resources and tools.

Get out of the habit of doing things that kill time instead of rediscovering it. Live in the present. Enjoy your Time-Wealth; go create the world you want to live in. If you're feeling overwhelmed remember, activity is the best cure for fear. If you start doubting yourself, the best thing you can do is to just get moving. I leave you with a final thought of my own in which I hope you find perpetual value.

"An ounce of action defeats a pound of doubt."

Epilogue

Notes from the Author

What allows us, as human beings, to psychologically survive on earth, with all its pain, drama, and challenges, is a sense of purpose and meaning.

> **- Barbara de Angelis, Bestselling Author and Psychologist**

I think Man has become very confused by wealth in the modern age. Just look at the marketing we are bombarded with – constant commercials of all the shiny things we "must have" modeled to us by the fashionable and beautiful. Funny how so little of that marketing includes an awareness of the Time-Wealth we need to actually enjoy such things.

I'm not suggesting that the toys we want are all meaningless. I don't have many material things in my life that I place much value on beyond some books that made a big impact on me, and a few sentimental gifts people have given to me throughout the years. Most of which would easily fit into half a dozen boxes. Let's face it though, you likely have a lot of crap laying around your house that you haven't used or even touched in years. Like I'd mentioned, I have a collection of books and even though I get a lot of enjoyment from them, if one has sat on my shelf for too long I consider if I really need to hang onto it.

Recently, on my way home from the store, both of my sons were upset because I refused to buy them something. I really don't remember what it was, and I'm sure they don't remember either, but I knew if I bought it – like 98% of their other toys – it would end up lost, broken or left outside in the rain within three days. I asked them both a question, and my wife, Jennifer, was given a chance to answer as well.

"Boys, what did we do last summer?" I asked.

Grumpy, they didn't want to play along. I said again:

"Boys, what are some of the things we did last summer?"

Begrudgingly, they started out, but they couldn't think of anything offhand, it was too far out of context for them.

"Did we drive on a long trip anywhere?" I asked, greasing the skids a little bit for them.

"Oh yeah!" said my oldest. "We went to New York to visit Uncle John, Aunt Sue, Eliza and Sydney!"

"That's right," I answered back. "And what are some of the things we did there?"

"We went on the boat and did that tubing thing on the water. Plus, we got to stay in the lake house. That was really neat."

My youngest, Logan, chimed in, "We got to roast marshmallows and make smores by the fire down by the lake."

"That's true Logan, I almost forgot about that." I said. "Do you guys remember stopping at Cabela's? I love that place." Everyone collectively agreeing.

Jennifer then added, "And remember the ride back when I had to pee in the bushes because nothing was open?"

All of us were hysterically laughing, reminiscing that part of the trip. There were several other memories of our visit, but I stopped there so I could make my point.

"Yeah that was a fun trip. Okay, now let me ask you something else. Name one thing that we bought for you on that trip."

The car was silent for a moment. I figured I'd have to give them a hint again, since the question required some thought.

"Do you guys remember going to that outdoor flea market?"

Still nothing.

"How about what we bought at Cabela's?"

Silence.

"Guys, you give so much value to the nonsense in our lives and not enough to the experiences we share." I said to them. "Leland and Logan, remember that we bought you those pocket knives at Cabela's you insisted on having?"

Both said "Yes," one at a time.

"Do you even know where they are?" I asked.

"Um, I think so," said one. "Maybe," said the other.

"And how much other crap have we bought since then?" I pressed, "In fact, name just one thing that we bought you just last month." I stopped and let them think.

I let the silence permeate through the vehicle. I had made my point.

I don't mean to sound so self-righteous, I've been through my own phase of more-more-more, especially as a kid. I think we all go through it, but some of us, in fact *many* of us, never seem to grow out of it. I am not trying to turn my kids into possession-less monks, I just want them to place value on the experiences and things in life that are worth valuing.

Of course, there is nearly always room for tools and gadgets in our lives that are part of our vision of the future. However, the boat you spent a fortune making payments on is meaningless if it's going to sit in your driveway 98% of the time. I have a desire to own an airplane, not because it's cool to say I own one, but because my wife and I plan to travel a lot and we would use it like a second car.

You must be the change you want to see in the world.

- Mahatma Gandhi

Creating the World You Want to Live In

Time-Wealth is not shiny nor is it easy to market or package with a label. Time-Wealth forces you to think in ways that reject the socially-approved "busy" lifestyle in favor of one that frees your time to do what is important to *you,* not what is deemed to be important by marketing executives that parade the latest dross in front of you. When you're already moving, in this case working, it's much easier to continue doing what you're already doing than it is to hop off the train and find something else to occupy your time.

In my 20s and 30s, I worked nearly non-stop because I thought I enjoyed work. What changed in me was facing the reality of the people around me dying with the best years of their lives still to live. I made a promise to myself and resolved that I wasn't going to let any more time go by without setting my sights on something worth doing every single day.

> **All we have to decide is what to do with the time that is given to us.**
>
> **- Gandalf, from *Lord of the Rings: The Fellowship of the Ring***

It doesn't take much to have a profound effect on the world around you. In my own case, I learned this to be true. Time-Wealth enabled me to start a veterans' event called "Standing for the Fallen." Started as a fundraiser, I would don my Marine Dress Blues and stand at attention at a chosen location somewhere in America. My mission was to raise money for Soldier's Angels, an organization devoted to the support of active duty military. Specifically, donations were raised for the injured and wounded who were sent to the Landstuhl military hospital in Germany. The money was used to purchase and ship comfort items such as calling cards, sweatpants, and zippered hoodies.

These events were as simple as they were effective. Standing at attention for 6 to 8 hours at a time, moving only to salute those that sounded their car horns in support, enabled me and my supporters to raise just over $100,000 in donations in just four years. I could never have pulled that off without the support of many amazing patriots that helped me along the way, and I'm forever in their debt. I also could never have pulled this off had I not had the ability to control my calendar. Time-Wealth enabled me to do this.

Ideas don't have to be physically taxing; consider the "You've Been Gifted" Project I recently started. A simple idea of paying it forward and providing an online mechanism, via a Facebook page, for people to chronicle their experiences. The idea is that someone would do a random act of kindness, whether paying for someone's coffee behind you in the drive-thru or mowing your neighbor's lawn, and leaving a 3x5 You've Been Gifted card behind so the recipient could then share their gift on the Facebook page. The card could then be reused to pay it forward to someone else. It's silly and some may even find it annoying. It's not meant to change the world, just my little piece of it. How you use your own Time-Wealth, is entirely up to you.

About the Author:

Mark Dolfini is a veteran of the U.S. Marines. He received a Bachelor of Science in Accounting at Purdue University, and worked for Marriott International before venturing out full-time in the world of real estate investing. He is the Managing Broker for June Palms Property Management, LLC, the CEO of Landlord Coach, LLC, and sits on numerous boards including the Better Business Bureau of Central Indiana, the National Federation of Independent Business, and is an Area Director for the Central Indiana BNI Franchise – a networking organization. He and his wife Jennifer live in Lafayette where they are raising their two sons, Leland and Logan.

Resources:

Scaling Up, by Verne Harnish

The E-Myth Revisited, by Michael Gerber

Good to Great, by Jim Collins

The 4-Hour Workweek, by Timothy Ferriss

The Power of Body Language, by Tonya Reiman

Instant Rapport, by Michael Brooks

The 7 Habits of Highly Successful People, by Steven Covey

The Magic of Thinking Big, by David Schwartz

The Ultimate Sales Machine, by Chet Holmes

The Effective Executive, by Peter Drucker

Sun Tzu and the Art of Business, by Mark McNeilly

Accounting: The Super-Duper Fun Part of Starting a Business, by Tressa Heath

Accounting Questions came from Kimberley Morisette, a partner at the Lafayette-based accounting firm of Huth Thompson, LLP and Becky Lively, an Indianapolis-based CPA.

Made in the USA
Monee, IL
25 February 2023

28373892R00164